The perfect meat is not VEALy the one that costs the most. The PORKfect meat is the one where you MEAT up with others and eat in good company!

Carnivore

Published originally in French (Canada) under the title: *Carnivore — Secrets de boucherie pour des cuissons parfaites*
© 2025, Les Éditions de l'Homme, a division of Groupe Sogides inc., a subsidiary of Québecor Media inc.
(Montréal, Québec, Canada)
English translation © 2025, Robert Rose Inc.

Library and Archives Canada Cataloguing in Publication
Title: Carnivore : a butcher's secrets for perfectly cooked meats / Dominique Rioux.
Other titles: Carnivore. English
Names: Rioux, Dominique, author.
Description: Includes index. | Translation of: Carnivore: secrets de boucherie pour des cuissons parfaites.
Identifiers: Canadiana 20250167514 | ISBN 9780778807377 (hardcover)
Subjects: LCSH: Cooking (Meat) | LCGFT: Cookbooks.
Classification: LCC TX749 .R5613 2025 | DDC 641.6/6—dc23

Disclaimer
Some recipes contain raw eggs. If you are concerned about the food safety of raw eggs, substitute pasteurized eggs in the shell or ¼ cup (60 mL) pasteurized liquid whole eggs for each egg you use.

Biscoff is a registered trademark of Lotus Bakeries.

Maggi is a registered trademark of Nestlé.

Editor: Marianne Prairie
Editor (English): Amy Treadwell
Translator: Anne Louise Mahoney
Copy editing: Lucie Desaulniers
Proofreading: Sylvie Massariol
Proofreading (English): Kelly Jones
Indexer (English): Gillan Watts
Photography: Ariel Tarr
Food styling: Dominique Rioux
Cooking and food styling assistance: Chantal Legault
Cover and graphic design: Clémence Beaudoin
Image processing: Johanne Lemay
Layout and production (English): PageWave Graphics Inc.

We acknowledge the support of the Government of Canada.

Canadä

Published by Robert Rose Inc.
120 Eglinton Avenue East, Suite 800, Toronto, Ontario, Canada M4P 1E2
Tel: (416) 322-6552 Fax: (416) 322-6936
www.robertrose.ca

Printed and bound in China

1 2 3 4 5 6 7 8 9 ESP   33 32 31 30 29 28 27 26 25

DOMINIQUE RIOUX

CARNIVORE

A BUTCHER'S SECRETS FOR PERFECTLY COOKED MEATS

Robert
ROSE

TABLE OF CONTENTS

POULTRY 177

FARMED GAME 205

APPENDICES 216

For Thiago Martinez Rioux . . .
Your auntie wants you to
believe in your dreams.
XOX

ABOUT

THE AUTHOR

Dominique Rioux eats a lot of meat! Cooking, barbecuing and butchering are not just her passions, they are her way of life. A real carnivore at heart, she has loved to cook and eat all kinds of meat since she was a child. In 2013, she got a degree in retail butchering from Montreal's culinary arts school. The only woman in her class, she received an award of excellence. Since then, Dominique has made several TV appearances, and in 2021, she charmed us with her porchetta on *Curieux Bégin* (*Curious Bégin*, Télé-Québec). Then, in 2024, she showed us how to make paupiettes in *La cuisine d'Isabelle et Ricardo* (*Isabelle and Ricardo's kitchen*, on Radio-Canada). She was a finalist at the televised contest *La coupe BBQ* (Zeste télé/TVA), where she went head to head with renowned chefs. The 2019 winner of Montreal's *Burger Week* with her humongous "sugar shack" burger, she has also hosted "Butcher's secrets" workshops as part of the YUL EAT festival. In 2025, she won the prestigious Laurier du Public award at the Lauriers de la gastronomie québécoise (public's choice.)

Dominique enjoys popularizing and sharing the knowledge she has gained over the years. Because of the way she stands out from the crowd and shatters stereotypes, she has won a large community of followers on social media. And because she's resourceful, she learned how to photograph, do video editing and build a website with her cellphone. Now she has learned how to write a book!

For Dom, it's important to be true to herself. For a long time, going off the beaten path was a source of suffering for her; now, it's one of her strengths, and she's very proud of it.

Where there's meat, there's hope!

Follow her on social media!
Website: www.dominique-rioux.com
Instagram: @dominique.rioux
TikTok: @dominique.rioux
Facebook: www.facebook.com/dominique.rioux.927

INTRODUCTION

ONCE UPON A TIME . . .

. . . there was a butcher who was very pleased to present her book to you!

Over the years, the art of butchering has really evolved in North America. The dawn of social media and access to world cuisine have greatly contributed to the emergence of new methods and trends when it comes to meat. Some cuts that used to be turned into ground meat are now very popular. I'm thinking of beef sirloin bavette (or flap): not long ago, it would automatically be ground. Today, it is a top choice for grilling. That's also why we've seen its price go up in recent years.

Meat cut terminology — the many names used for butcher's cuts — can be intimidating for a lot of people. French cuts are different from cuts in Canada, the US and elsewhere. Sometimes, even within a country, certain cuts have different names depending on the region!

This book is designed as a simple guide, a "mini bible" for everyone who eats meat: everyday cooks, chefs, butchers, barbecue enthusiasts, students and new butcher shop staff. It's for people who love to cook and even those who don't love to cook! In addition to information and tips, I offer you a wide range of recipes that are as varied as they are tasty.

After more than 10 years as a butcher, I have learned to listen to the customers and to guide them in their different meat-shopping needs. The same questions come up often — almost all the time. Below, I give clear answers to your questions . . . with a bit of personality, of course! Exactly as if I were the one standing behind the butcher's counter.

Question 1. How do I cook the piece of meat I have?

You can look in the table of contents for a particular type of meat, then go to the page indicated. There you will find the best way to cook it (there's even more info on cooking methods on page 13). Which brings me to the next question . . .

Question 2. What other cut could I use instead of stewing cubes?

Once you have identified a cut and its best cooking method, you can decide to replace it with another cut that requires a similar cooking method, making it easy and economical to use what you have on hand or in the freezer. For example, why buy stewing cubes for a beef bourguignon if you already have a blade chuck roast (bottom blade pot roast) that you bought on sale waiting in the freezer? Just cut it into cubes and you're done!

Question 3. My recipe from France calls for gîte de bœuf. I tried five butchers, but no luck. Where can I find it?

The Meat Translator chart starting on page 216 will help you identify a cut that could go by several names. It will give the name used in the US, in English Canada, Quebec and France, as well as any other English terms used for this cut. Answer: gîte de bœuf is the same as shank in English.

Question 4. What part of the animal does this steak I've been eating every Friday for 10 years come from?

Each chapter starts with anatomical drawings to show you where the wholesale and retail cuts of each animal are found.

Another im-PORK-tant aim for me was to give you as many recipes as possible. Recipes for all tastes: from simple to impressive, for weeknights to long weekends, for the barbecue, the smoker or the stove, for amateurs or professionals, for kids or adults, and much more. There is a stew cooked in a pumpkin and a Thor's hammer beef shank that is lit like a candle. The sky's the limit! I think it's essential to provide recipes in smaller quantities, because I often hear from people who live alone who tell me: "I like cooking for other people, but I don't really cook when it's just me at home." I want to give them the option of taking time to cook for themselves, because they deserve good meals, too!

Finally, as you've probably noticed already, I throw in a few puns here and there. My philosophy is that it's important to laugh and have fun when you're cooking and butchering . . . and in everything you do, VEALy!

The meat cuts in this book are based on French-Canadian artisan butchery cuts, sometimes enriched with European French artisan butchery cuts, and they don't always match up exactly to US or Canadian English-language meat cuts and standard terminology. The appendix at the back of the book will help guide you, providing translations and possible alternate names for cuts, and you can visit your local butcher who may be able to help answer your questions.

TABLES FOR CUTS

AND COOKING METHODS

For each animal, I've included a diagram of the wholesale cuts. Then, in a table, I've specified which retail cuts can be made from these parts and the best cooking methods for preparing them. Sometimes I add small muscles of interest for you to get to know!

Basic definitions of cooking methods are:

Braise Sear (or not) the food on all sides in sizzling fat, then add a small amount of liquid to the pan, cover and cook over low heat.

Fry In a skillet, over high or medium-high heat, cook the food in a small amount of very hot oil (or other fat). Alternatively, you can deep-fry by immersing the food in hot oil to cook it.

Grill Cook the food through direct contact with the heat source. This includes cooking on the barbecue, under the oven broiler and in a non-stick grill pan without fat.

Raw All meats eaten raw, such as tartare and carpaccio. Tataki can also be included in this category.

Roast Sear (or not) the food on all sides in sizzling fat, then place in the oven, uncovered, without adding any liquid.

Sauté In a skillet, over high heat, cook the food very quickly while stirring vigorously.

Simmer Immerse the food in a cold liquid of your choice. Bring to a boil and then reduce the heat to maintain a simmer until fully cooked.

When you know the appropriate cooking method for each cut, you can easily choose any type of meat that will work for the same type of cooking. The recipe for beef shank can be made with a pot roast, stew cubes, brisket or any other stewing cut. You get the idea. All you need to do is adjust the cooking time based on the size of the piece of meat. You can have fun, save money and adapt with no problem!

MEAT

BASIC PRINCIPLES

In the world of butchering, some basic information is a must to become familiar with meat and learn how to prepare it. In the pages that follow, you will discover more about how to become a carnivore expert. And that's no misSTEAK!

Osteology

This part of the anatomy involves the bones and skeleton of the animal. Here we find landmarks for the various wholesale cuts and for each retail cut, which is very important for butchering. Osteology is a bit like street names on a map: when you want to identify meat cuts, it really helps to understand where they are found and what they are made of. To make it easier for you to visualize, I've included the different osteologies of quadrupeds and poultry on pages 230 and 232.

Tender and less tender cuts

To put it simply, the more a muscle is used by an animal, the less tender the meat will be, therefore it should be cooked longer, in recipes like stews. These cuts do tend to have a deeper flavor. The more tender cuts are often considered "premium" because they come from parts that the animal uses less, and will be perfect for grilling or pan frying. These tender cuts typically have a milder flavor. If you think about it, an animal works exactly like a car with front-wheel drive. The front of the animal works hard so the back can follow with less effort. This means less tender cuts are found mainly at the front and part of the back of the animal, while more tender cuts are mostly along the backbone and toward the back — with a few exceptions, which you will learn about in due course.

> **Fun fact:** the tenderloin steak (often referred to as filet mignon), the most tender muscle of the carcass (although it doesn't have a lot of flavor), is found in the loin, with a small portion of the sirloin, whose job is to tilt the pelvis during reproduction. This muscle doesn't get much use in animals being fattened for food (rather than for breeding), which is why it's so tender. What about you: is your filet mignon tender?

Fat

Meat contains three kinds of fat: external (subcutaneous) fat, marbling (intramuscular) and seam fat (intermuscular). While external fat covers the muscle, marbling is found within the muscle fibers themselves. This type of fat melts during cooking, which makes it an excellent indicator of quality. Beef grading is done using these criteria:

- **USDA Standard/Canada A:** None to trace fat (very little marbling)
- **USDA Select/Canada AA:** Slight (a little marbling)
- **USDA Choice/Canada AAA:** Small to moderate (a lot of marbling)
- **USDA Prime/Canada Prime:** Slightly abundant to abundant (extremely marbled — close to heaven for meat lovers)

Seam fat separates the muscles. It requires a higher temperature and longer cooking time before it melts and is pleasant to chew.

The makeup of the cut indicates the ideal way to cook it

The arrangement of the muscles and fat (and the proportions of the two) offers very good indications of the best way to cook the meat. Let's compare two pieces of beef that require two completely different cooking methods given their makeup: a ribeye (rib eye) and a strip (strip loin).

A chuck eye steak (also called Delmonico), contains four muscles separated by fat. This cut requires a higher internal temperature to allow the fat between the muscles to melt to give a pleasant texture in the mouth during chewing. That's why it is rarely recommended that it be eaten blue or rare. The strip steak (strip loin steak), on the other hand, contains a large central muscle covered by a layer of surface fat as well as the eye, a tiny muscle surrounded by fat. This cut can be eaten very rare, blue or even prepared as a tataki. Given that there is almost no fat — except on the surface — it becomes less enjoyable to chew when cooked beyond rare. That said, it's a question of what you're used to and personal preference.

Tempering meat

Tempering helps the meat to transition between cold (refrigerated) and hot (grill or skillet) without causing a too sudden change in temperature. When you examine a piece of cooked meat, you can definitely notice a major difference when it has been tempered beforehand. This is due to the fact that meat that is at room temperature will sear much more quickly, without cooling down the heat source used for cooking. This will give the surface a nice crisp, even crunchy texture. A golden and delicious crust is created following a chain of chemical reactions between amino acids and sugars, called the Maillard reaction, which is responsible for the browning of meat during cooking. Keep in mind that for food safety, meat should never be left at room temperature more than 2 hours, or 1 hour if the room is greater than 90°F (32°C). Ground or mechanically tenderized meats should never be tempered (USDA).

Tempering also helps to relax muscle fibers and tissues, unlike cold, which causes them to contract. Also, when it comes to flavor, meat flavors are released at room temperature, a little like cheese that you bring to room temperature before eating. Generally, the meats to temper are those you can eat slightly pink or rare: beef, veal and lamb. Only one type of poultry is tempered: duck. Never temper other types of poultry.

Start with salt, then add other seasonings

As you will see when you get to the recipes later in the book, most of the time, the only spice I put on the meat before searing is salt. Roasted spices bring a ton of flavors, of course, but at this stage, spices will burn because of the intense heat and will not taste good. For example, pepper and mustard become very bitter. Another problem with seasoning first is that you will not be searing the meat but the spices covering it. I therefore prefer to season after the meat is nicely browned.

When to use direct and indirect cooking

These two types of cooking, while very different, are often complementary. Direct cooking, as the name implies, is done directly over the heat source to grill and brown the meat (or other food). With indirect cooking, the heat source is close by but not in direct contact with the meat. It does not directly lead to browning and allows you to cook the piece to the center without overcooking the outside. Here's a simple example: On the stove, we sear meat in a skillet to brown it (direct cooking) and finish cooking in the oven (indirect cooking). For steaks and roasts, cooking indirectly over low heat, 250°F (125°C), gives a sous vide (vacuum) cooking effect, so the center of the meat is more uniformly cooked.

On a grill, different methods can be used for these two types of cooking. If using a gas grill, light only one side of the grill for direct cooking; the other side will be used for indirect cooking. If using charcoal, place hot coals on one side of the barbecue, so you get direct cooking over or directly on the coals, and indirect cooking on the side away from the heat.

Note: two methods (or steps) are often used to cook meat: direct-indirect or indirect-direct. The first involves searing the meat directly and then finishing the cooking indirectly. The second involves cooking indirectly, then searing the meat at the end (this is called "reverse sear"). I mostly cook with charcoal, so it's more practical for me to use the first technique, as it allows me to make only one charcoal chimney instead of having to prepare a second one to sear my meat. I have done many tests: the two approaches are similar — almost identical.

Let the meat rest

Just like tempering raw meat is worthwhile, letting cooked meat rest is also very imPORKtant! When meat is cooking, the heat activates the molecules of various internal juices. You won't notice it, but when you grill a steak, there is quite a party going on inside that piece of meat!

That's why it's essential to let the meat rest after cooking to preserve these interior juices when it's time to carve. Cutting meat too quickly will mean losing these delectable juices on the plate. We want them to stay inside the meat and give a pleasing texture and flavor in the mouth. It's a bit like when we stand up too fast and feel a bit dizzy: we need some time between sitting and standing to get our balance. It's the same for meat after cooking. We need to give it time to adjust and find its balance between two states: cooking and non-cooking. For this reason, a piece of meat that rests after cooking will be PORKfect. The moral of the story: a little snooze and you can't lose!

The direction of meat fibers

This section does not concern meats that are shredded, but rather those that are sliced. When it's time to serve a roast, a steak or even a chicken breast, it is important to cut perpendicular to the direction of the meat fibers. To put it more simply, the knife should make an X across the fibers, which will shorten them and naturally separate the fibers. This makes the meat easier to chew and gives it a nice feel in the mouth. BEEFore you slice, place your knife in the right direction!

Aging of meat

Contrary to popular belief, the meat you buy at the butcher's or at the grocery store isn't from an animal that was butchered the day before. Meat, primarily beef, that is too freshly butchered doesn't have a pleasant texture or flavor at all. It is even considered inedible! The aging in the first few days (7 to 10 days) helps to relax the nerves, muscle fibers and tissues to make the meat edible. Aging can extend beyond this period, especially to tenderize the meat and develop a somewhat nutty flavor. The more a piece of meat or carcass ages, the more pronounced this distinctive flavor will be and the more tender the meat will be . . . but you will also need to remove more of the rind, a coating that is often black (called the pellicle), which reduces the meat yield over time (and explains the higher price of aged meat). That's why 30 to 60 days of aging is suggested to get an optimal result without too much loss. Some people will age their meat as much as 2 to 3 years to get a stronger flavor. At this point, only a very small amount is edible after the rind is removed. Enthusiasts enjoy the taste of aged meat, but for many people, the flavor is too different from "regular" beef. We can roughly compare this kind of appreciation to that of mild Cheddar (like meat that has not been aged long) versus that of blue cheese (like aged meat). Many people like Cheddar but don't necessarily like the taste of blue cheese.

A MEAT THERMOMETER

IS A MUST

To find out the internal temperature, insert the thermometer in the thickest part of the meat, right to the center. To get the most accurate reading, make sure you don't touch bone on the way through. For larger cuts, I recommend a model with a probe that can be used in the oven and on the barbecue. It stays in the meat and indicates the temperature precisely throughout cooking, in real time. An instant-read thermometer is used to test at the end of cooking.

Recommended internal temperatures

Beef, veal, lamb – pieces and whole cuts
Blue: 120°F (50°C)
Extra rare: 130°F (54°C)
Rare: 140°F (60°C)
Medium-rare: 145°F (63°C)
Medium: 160°F (71°C)
Well done: 170°F (77°C)
Very well done: 180°F (82°C)

Game – pieces, whole cuts and ground: 165°F (74°C)

Ground meat and mechanically-tenderized meat (beef, veal, lamb): 160°F (71°C)

Pork – pieces, including mechanically tenderized, whole cuts and ground: 160°F (71°C)

Poultry – pieces, ground and whole birds: 165°F (74°C)

The temperature will continue to rise 5°F to 10°F (3°C to 6°C), depending on the size of the meat or poultry, when the food is removed from the oven or barbecue, so it is best to remove it when the internal temperature is slightly less than the desired temperature.

Beef

Beef is one of the most consumed meats in the world. Tasty, full of nutrients and very versatile for cooking, it can be eaten raw, cooked, dried or smoked. Beef cuts are classified into three categories: premium, secondary and third. Premium is mainly made up of beef for grilling, from the rib, the loin, as well as the round and hip. Shoulder cuts are classified as secondary, while third category cuts, which are tougher and need more cooking time, include the brisket, the shanks and the neck and are often used in stews. The classification of the meat is no indication of its flavor and, in fact, all categories of meat contain delicious options.

A whole beef tenderloin weighs about 6 lbs (2.8 kg), while a whole lamb tenderloin is less than 7 oz (200 g). A cow's massive size is also one of the reasons why beef is dealt with in quarters by butchers, unlike lamb and pork, which are handled as an entire carcass. Given that the weight of a whole carcass is around 1000 lbs (450 k), beef has more cuts than any other animal used in the food industry.[1]

In the cattle family, there are two types of breeds: dairy cattle for milk production and beef cattle for eating, such as Galloway, Limousin, Charolais, Black Angus, Red Angus, Blonde d'Aquitaine, Hereford, Highland, Texas Longhorn and Wagyu. Tajima is used for Kobe beef, the well-known designation raised in Japan. Holy cow — that's a lot of beef!

---

1 These are trades related to the preparation of products and foods for human consumption, such as chef, butcher, chocolatier, fishmonger and baker.

BEEF

FOREQUARTER BEEF CUTS

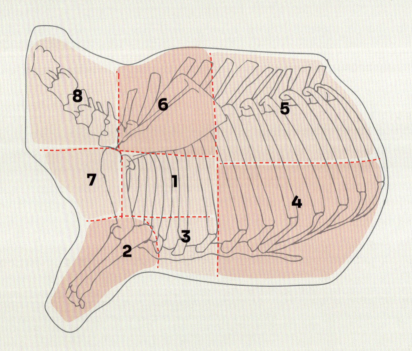

1 – CROSS RIB   5 – RIB

2 – SHANK (FRONT)   6 – BLADE

3 – BRISKET   7 – SHOULDER BONE

4 – PLATE   8 – NECK

1 – CROSS RIB

The cross rib, which the animal relies on to move around, is the source of retail meat cuts that are not very tender but are very tasty — they simply require longer cooking times. The shoulder cross rib contains the central part of the first five ribs, a piece of the humerus and the scapulo-humeral joint. In general, these muscles are perfect for simmering or braising.

For connoisseurs: In the shoulder clod, we find the shoulder petite tender (shoulder clod petite tender) which may also be referred to *teres major*, a delicious and tender muscle because it is one that the animal uses less. It can be enjoyed as a steak, in tataki or even tartare.

WHOLESALE CUT: CROSS RIB	
Retail cut	**Cooking method**
Shoulder clod steak	Grill, simmer, sauté
Chuck short ribs	Braise, simmer, roast
Short ribs (sliced)	Grill, sauté, marinate
Stew cubes	Simmer
Lean stew cubes	Simmer
Cross rib roast - *Individual muscle: deep pectoral*	Braise, simmer, roast *Raw, grill, sauté*
Shoulder clod roast (tenderized or not) - *Individual muscle: shoulder petite tender*	Braise, simmer, roast *Raw, grill, sauté*

2 – SHANK (FRONT)

Directly connected to the shoulder bone, the shank (specifically the foreshank) is an ideal cut for pot-au-feu, stew and slow, low-heat cooking in the oven, on the barbecue or even in a smoker. A specific feature of this cut is its bone with marrow in the center, as well as a variety of small muscles filled with collagen that surround it. Collagen is an ally for stews, giving texture to sauces and tenderizing meat as it melts during cooking. Marrow brings flavor. The marrow can also be used in different recipes, especially roasted and eaten on bread, as you would use butter.

WHOLESALE CUT: SHANK (FRONT)	
Retail cut	**Cooking method**
Stew cubes	Simmer
Shank center-cut (sliced or whole)	Braise, simmer
Boneless shank (tied or not)	Braise, simmer
Rolled boneless shank	Braise, simmer
Thor's hammer (Frenched shank)	Braise, simmer
Marrow bones; canoe cut or cross cut	Braise, grill, simmer, roast

These two primal cuts are very similar; the brisket is closer to the front with the plate positioned between the brisket and the flank (in the hindquarter). The plate contains ribs and rib cartilage as well as muscle that extends from the brisket plus the outside skirt. We find the short ribs in the plate as well (they are an extension of the bones of the rib primal cut). The brisket primal cut is made up of sternebrae, ribs and rib cartilage and large muscles. The muscles in the brisket and plate are very flavorful but not very tender, they work well in recipes that are cooked slowly over low heat or simmered. The brisket is the cut that is often used for Montreal smoked meat and for Texas-style barbecued brisket or corned beef.

More info: In the US and often in Canada, the muscle from the brisket primal cut is considered to be a whole brisket (see photo on page 25) though there is an extension of the muscle that goes into the plate primal cut. In the brisket, there are two muscles which are often separated: the smaller muscle is called the point (also called the double or deckle) and the large, flat muscle is called the flat. While people love brisket cooked on the barbecue or in the smoker, it is also delicious braised in the oven or simmered as a pot roast or stew.

Even more info: Here is a perfect example of how butchering has evolved over the years. Brisket cut in the US style (with just the portion from the brisket primal) has won over meat lovers in Canada, making it commonly available. In the classic Canadian cut, a whole brisket includes the brisket (point and flat portions) plus the extension of the flat found in the plate primal cut.

WHOLESALE CUT: BRISKET	
Retail cut	**Cooking method**
Whole brisket	Braise, simmer
Stew cubes	Simmer
Brisket point, whole or in pieces	Braise, simmer
Brisket flat, whole or in pieces	Braise, simmer
Strips	Grill, simmer, sauté

WHOLESALE CUT: PLATE	
Retail cut	**Cooking method**
Flanken style short ribs	Braise, grill, simmer, sauté
Plate short ribs	Braise, simmer
Crown of short ribs	Braise, simmer
Outside skirt	Raw, grill, sauté
Stew cubes	Simmer
Strips	Grill, sauté
Boneless plate (rolled or not)	Braise, grill (sometimes, simmer)

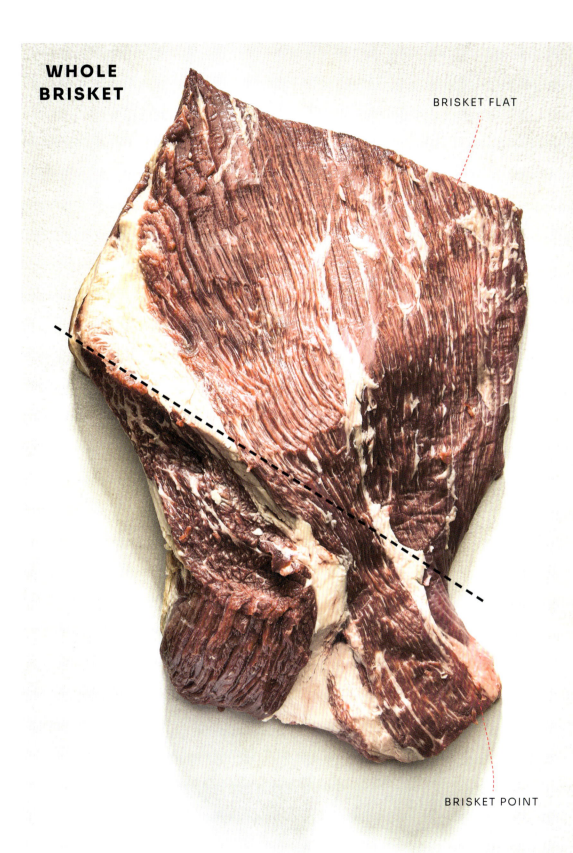

WHOLE
BRISKET

BRISKET FLAT

BRISKET POINT

The rib primal cut gets its name from the fact that the cut contains ribs from one end to the other (7 ribs). Found behind the chuck and near the spine, these muscles do very little work. Whether as a steak or a roast, these cuts are not only very tasty but very tender, too. It's the most prestigious wholesale cut in the beef forequarter. It contains highly valued cuts such as the prime rib roast or rib steak (bone in) and the ribeye roast or steak (boneless) — called entrecôte in France — which are actually the same piece cut with and without the bone. To make a tomahawk steak, all you need to do is keep the full length of the bone on a rib steak. For a cowboy steak (Frenched rib steak), you leave less of the bone: about 2 inches (5 cm). Broadly speaking, these four retail cuts (tomahawk, ribeye, prime rib and cowboy steak) include exactly the same muscles: the difference is in how the bone is dealt with.

For connoisseurs: The rib has three parts:
1 The chuck part, near the blade, is fattier, with four separate muscles (see photo, page 27), including the spinalis (the ribeye cap), which is at its largest in this section. Meat lovers adore it!
2 The loin end is leaner, as it is an extension of the sirloin.
3 The center part is nicely balanced between the blade and the loin: not too fatty and not too lean.

More info: Along the spine, inside the chest wall, is a fat called beef suet, which covers part of the kidneys. Attached to them is the hanger steak, one of the tastiest muscles of the carcass.

WHOLESALE CUT: RIB	
Retail cut	**Cooking method**
Back ribs	Braise, grill, simmer, roast
Beef suet (inside the chest wall)	see box (page 29)
Cowboy steak (Frenched rib steak)	Grill, sauté
Hanger steak	Raw, grill, sauté
Prime rib roast	Braise, roast
Ribeye roast	Braise, roast
Ribeye steak (boneless)	Grill, sauté
Rib short ribs	Braise, simmer
Rib short ribs (sliced or grilling)	Braise, grill, simmer, sauté
Rib steak (bone in) - *Individual muscle: complexus* - *Individual muscle: longissimus dorsi (loin)* - *Individual muscle: hanger (inside the chest wall)* - *Individual muscle: spinalis (ribeye cap)*	Grill, sauté *Raw, grill, sauté* *Raw, grill, sauté* *Raw, grill, sauté* *Grill, sauté*
Tomahawk steak	Grill, sauté

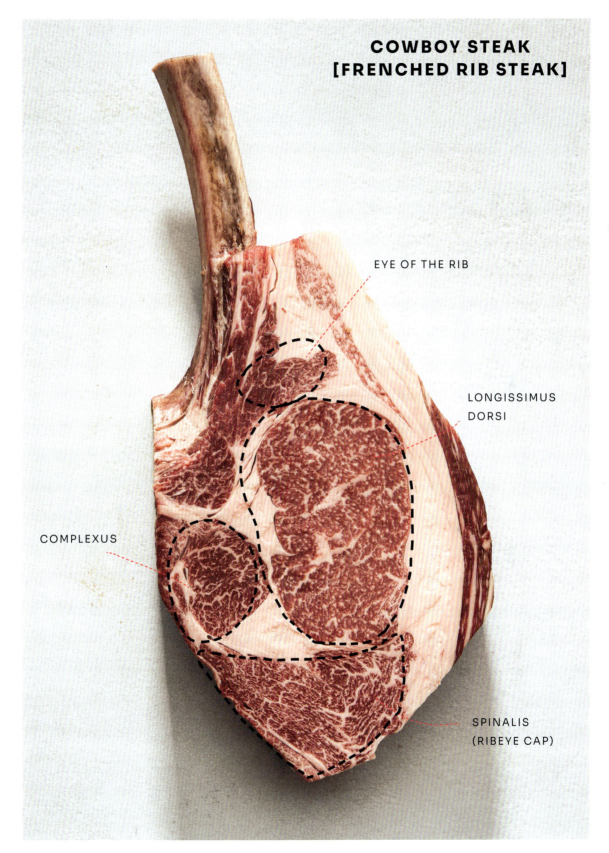

COWBOY STEAK
[FRENCHED RIB STEAK]

EYE OF THE RIB

LONGISSIMUS
DORSI

COMPLEXUS

SPINALIS
(RIBEYE CAP)

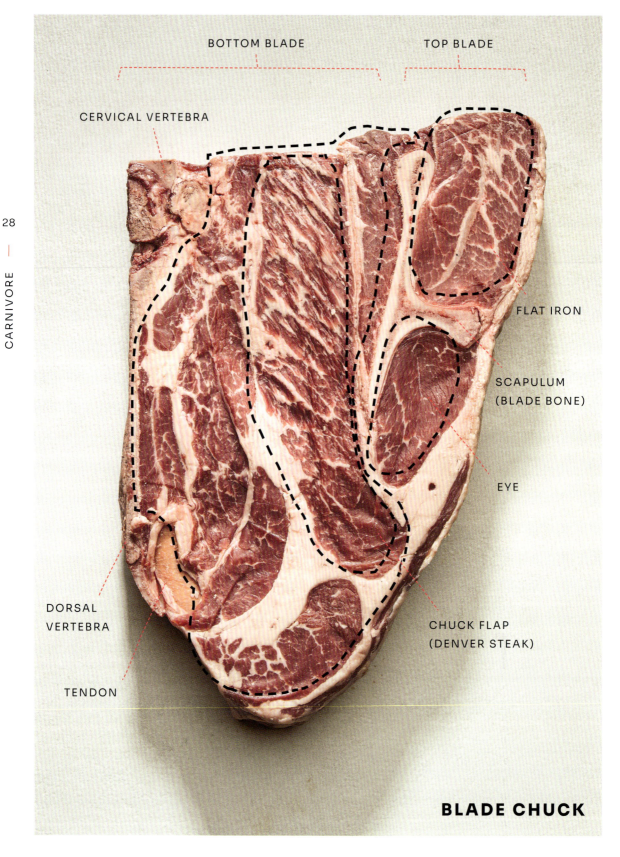

BOTTOM BLADE

TOP BLADE

CERVICAL VERTEBRA

FLAT IRON

SCAPULUM
(BLADE BONE)

EYE

DORSAL
VERTEBRA

CHUCK FLAP
(DENVER STEAK)

TENDON

BLADE CHUCK

BEEF SUET

Suet is fat found inside the chest wall that covers part of the kidneys. It is used as cooking fat for meat or vegetables, especially in Belgium to cook their famous fries! It is also popular at Christmas to make traditional plum pudding. Suet is a VERY tasty fat with a pronounced beef flavor. It is sometimes mistakenly called beef tallow, which is simply melted beef fat that does not necessarily come from suet.

6 – BLADE

This wholesale cut is found between the neck and rib. For many cooks, it is the cut of choice for fall and winter stews. The popular blade chuck roast (blade pot roast) is found in this wholesale cut. It's flavorful, though some would say it's even better reheated the next day! In stores, it's often found without the bone as boneless blade chuck roast (boneless bottom blade pot roast). The blade chuck roast (blade pot roast) with the bone in contains the top and bottom blade, the eye and the flat iron (see photo, page 28). The flat iron itself has two parts: the steak part and the stew/pot-au-feu part. It contains two parallel muscles separated by a nerve that, when it melts, creates collagen, which gives it that melt-in-your-mouth feel. It's the wild card of meat cuts: it becomes almost whatever you like!

For connoisseurs: In the center of the chuck roll (or bottom blade) is a large rectangular muscle that is often called the chuck flat (under blade or chuck flap tail). Both tasty and tender, this part is not expensive and is excellent as a grilled steak, and often called a Denver steak (you can also find an extension of that muscle in the plate). Also, the first slice (only) of the blade toward the rib can be cut as a chuck eye steak (also called the Delmonico steak) and grilled, as we do with a prime rib (though it's much more economical).

More info: Near the blade bone, you'll find a muscle called the surprise which is cut into steaks; it's a tender and satisfying cut for grilling.

WHOLESALE CUT: BLADE	
Retail cut	**Cooking method**
Chuck roll (bottom blade) - *Individual muscle: chuck flat/Denver steak*	Braise *Grill, sauté*
Chuck eye steak (Delmonico)	Grill, sauté
Boneless blade chuck roast (boneless bottom blade pot roast)	Braise, simmer
Top blade roast - *Individual muscle: the surprise* - *Individual muscle: flat iron (2 muscles)* - *Individual muscle: chuck eye*	Braise, simmer *Raw, grill, sauté* *Braise, grill, simmer, sauté* *Braise, simmer*
Blade chuck roast (blade pot roast)	Braise, simmer

7/8 – THE NECK AND THE SHOULDER BONE

The neck of the animal contains the vertebrae. The animal uses its neck constantly, whether for eating, drinking or moving its head, and though it's a very tasty cut, it does contain a lot of bones. That's why, most of the time, it is deboned and the meat is used to make stewing cubes and ground meat. It can be cooked with the bones but is not often found at the butcher in this form.

The shoulder bone (also called the round arm) connects the neck and the shank (foreshank) and contains one part of a large bone: the humerus. The muscles involved are also heavily used by the animal whenever it walks around or moves its head. Like the neck, it is usually deboned and cut into cubes, ground and, perhaps more rarely, sliced for stew or pot-au-feu.

WHOLESALE CUT: NECK + SHOULDER BONE	
Retail cut	**Cooking method**
Stew cubes	Braise, simmer
Lean cubes for stew	Braise, simmer
Sliced shoulder bone (pot-au-feu)	Braise, simmer

9 – HEAD

The head contains a number of muscles, which are often considered in the same category as offal. The cheeks among others, are used quite a lot by the animal, and they are full of collagen, very tender and so tasty when cooked! The meat fibers in beef cheeks are much finer than in most stewing cuts. Definitely a cut worth trying! The tongue tends to be overlooked; it deserves to be used more often in your stews.

WHOLESALE CUT: HEAD	
Retail cut	**Cooking method**
Jowls	Braise, simmer
Cheek	Braise, simmer
Tongue	Braise, grill, simmer

The meat cuts in this book are based on French-Canadian artisan butchery cuts, sometimes enriched with European French artisan butchery cuts, and they don't always match up exactly to US or Canadian English-language meat cuts and standard terminology. The appendix at the back of the book will help guide you, providing translations and possible alternate names for cuts, and you can visit your local butcher who may be able to help answer your questions.

BEEF TATAKI + LEMON + GREEN BEANS + GARLIC

Serves
2 reasonable eaters or
1 aggressive eater
Prep time – 20 min
Tempering – 30 min
Cooking time – 20 min

Tataki

1 whole beef shoulder petite tender
(shoulder clod petite tender), about
½ lb (250 g)
Salt
1 tbsp (15 mL) vegetable oil

Lemon poppyseed vinaigrette

½ cup (125 mL) vegetable oil
Zest of 1 lemon
¼ cup (60 mL) lemon juice
2 tbsp (30 mL) honey
1 tbsp (15 mL) Dijon mustard
1 tsp (5 mL) poppy seeds

Garlic green beans

2 tbsp (30 mL) vegetable oil
1 cup (250 mL) green beans
3 garlic cloves, shoots removed, crushed
3 tbsp (45 mL) butter
2 sprigs of fresh thyme (or your choice
of fresh herbs)
Salt and pepper

For serving (optional)

1 radish, thinly sliced
A few cucumber ribbons

1. **Tataki.** Unwrap the beef and let it sit at room temperature on a wire rack for 30 minutes.

2. Meanwhile, make the **lemon poppyseed vinaigrette**. In a jar with a lid, combine oil, lemon zest and juice, honey, mustard and poppy seeds. Close the lid and shake vigorously until the vinaigrette is smooth. Set aside.

3. Evenly salt the meat to your taste. In a skillet, over high heat, heat 1 tbsp (15 mL) oil and sear the meat on all sides. Let rest on a plate while you prepare the beans.

4. **Garlic green beans.** In the same skillet, over high heat, heat the oil and sauté the beans. Once they are browned, add the garlic, butter and thyme. Add salt and pepper to taste. Cook until the butter foams and turns brown; remove skillet from heat.

5. Cut the beef across the grain into thin slices. On the plates, arrange a few slices of tataki on top of the garlic green beans and serve with the lemon poppyseed vinaigrette. If desired, garnish with sliced radish and cucumber ribbons.

Note

To make this recipe on the grill, preheat gas grill to high or use a charcoal chimney starter to get glowing coals for a charcoal barbecue. Sear the meat over direct heat on the grill or directly on the coals. Also, make sure that the skillet you use for the beans is fire resistant!

BEEF SHANK + TOMATOES + WHITE WINE + VEGETABLES

Where the beef shank comes from: the shank (foreshank or hindshank)

Serves
6 prudent people or
4 fearless people
Prep time – 30 min
Tempering – 20 min
Cooking time – 4 to 6 hours

2 slices beef shank, about 1½ inches
  (4 cm) thick

2 tbsp (30 mL) vegetable oil

3 onions, diced

5 garlic cloves, shoots removed, finely
  chopped

3 tbsp (45 mL) all-purpose flour

1½ cups (375 mL) dry white wine

1 cup (250 mL) beef stock

1 can (14 oz/398 mL) diced tomatoes

3 sprigs of fresh thyme

1 tsp (5 mL) dried oregano

Salt and pepper to taste

5 carrots, peeled and cut in half
  lengthwise

12 baby potatoes

8 oz (227 g) white mushrooms, halved

1. Unwrap the beef and let sit at room temperature on a wire rack for 20 minutes.
2. Preheat the oven to 250°F (125°C).
3. In a Dutch oven or other oven-proof heavy, shallow saucepan, over high heat, heat the oil and sear the meat on all sides until browned. Set aside on a plate.
4. Add onions and garlic and sauté for 3 minutes, until browned. Sprinkle with flour; cook, stirring, for 1 minute.
5. Deglaze with the white wine, scraping the bottom with a wooden spoon to get all the brown bits. Add beef stock, tomatoes, thyme and oregano; bring to a simmer, while stirring. Add salt and pepper to your taste.
6. Stir in carrots and potatoes. Place the shanks on the vegetable mixture.
7. Cover and bake for about 5 hours or until the meat comes off the bone easily.
8. Stir in mushrooms and bake, uncovered, for 20 minutes.

Note
You can reduce the cooking time by increasing the oven temperature to 300°F (150°C) and baking for about 4 hours in step 7.

Notes

A whole brisket is pretty big (see page 25)! The recipe also works well with a half brisket of about 5½ lbs (2.5 kg), preferably the point for the extra fattiness, but the flat will work, too. There's no change to the ingredients or the steps in the process; simply use a little less of the flavor infusion to be injected.

Beef suet (see page 29) can be replaced by melted unsalted butter, but it shouldn't be too hot.

Brisket

One 11 lb (5 kg) whole beef brisket (see Notes)
Salt and pepper to taste
1 can (12 oz/355 mL) cola

Flavor infusion

2 cups (500 mL) unsalted beef stock
2 cups (500 mL) beef suet (see Notes)
½ cup (125 mL) soy sauce
1 can (5½ oz/156 mL) seasoned vegetable cocktail
½ cup (125 mL) Worcestershire sauce

Equipment

Syringe/injector
Smoking wood chips
Spray bottle
Butcher paper, foil or parchment paper
Meat thermometer

BRISKET + SMOKE + CHOLESTEROL

.
.
.

Where the whole brisket comes from: the brisket

Serves – about 15 people or the entire village
Prep time – 30 min   **Refrigeration** – 12 to 20 hours   **Tempering** – 1 hour
Cooking time – 8 to 10 hours   **Resting time** – 45 min

1. Brisket. If needed, trim off the fat from the brisket to taste.

2. Flavor infusion. In a bowl, combine beef stock, beef suet, soy sauce, vegetable cocktail and Worcestershire sauce until smooth.

3. With a syringe, inject the flavor infusion into the brisket every 1½ inches (4 cm) angling it in the direction of the meat fibers. You don't need to use the entire amount. Wrap the brisket in plastic wrap, place on a tray and let rest in the fridge for 12 to 20 hours.

4. Unwrap the brisket and let it sit at room temperature on a wire rack for 1 hour. With paper towel, sponge the excess liquid from the surface.

5. Meanwhile, preheat the smoker, charcoal barbecue or gas grill to between 250 and 275°F (125 and 135 °C). Once the internal temperature has been reached, add your choice of smoking wood and set up for indirect heat cooking, if necessary.

6. Season the brisket with salt and pepper to your taste. Place on the smoker, barbecue or grill over indirect heat.

7. Smoke the meat for about 4 hours or until the internal temperature reaches 175°F (80°C). Meanwhile, fill the spray bottle with cola and spray the brisket three or four times. To avoid a loss of smoke or variations in temperature, don't open the lid of the barbecue or smoker more than necessary (for spraying).

8. Remove the meat from the smoker or barbecue and place on a tray. Increase the temperature to 275°F (135°C).

9. Place a large sheet of butcher paper or parchment paper on a rimmed baking sheet; pour a little cola in the middle, then place the brisket on it. Seal the paper to make a pouch.

10. Slide the pouch off the baking sheet onto the grill and continue cooking with indirect heat for about 4 hours until the internal temperature reaches 190°F (93°C). The thermometer should go into the brisket as if it were butter. If this is not the case, continue cooking until it does.

11. Remove the meat from the heat, sliding the pouch back onto the baking sheet. Let rest in the paper for about 45 minutes.

12. Unwrap and transfer to a cutting board. Cut brisket across the grain into thin slices.

BEEF SHORT RIBS + RASPBERRIES + MAPLE + RICE NOODLES

Where the plate short ribs come from: the plate or rib

Serves
3 polite people or 2 impolite people
Prep time – 20 min
Tempering – 30 min
Cooking time – 5 hours 15 min

Short ribs

3 individual beef plate short ribs (see Notes)

Salt

3 tbsp (45 mL) vegetable oil

¾ cup (175 mL) raspberries, fresh or frozen

Maple sauce

¼ cup (60 mL) veal stock

3 onions, chopped

4 garlic cloves, shoots removed, chopped

¼ cup (60 mL) chopped fresh gingerroot

2 cups (500 mL) hoisin sauce

1 cup (250 mL) oyster sauce

1 cup (250 mL) pure maple syrup

3 tbsp (45 mL) toasted sesame oil

Hot pepper sauce (optional)

For serving

12 oz (375 g) wide rice noodles

Edamame, shelled and reheated

Green onions, finely chopped on the diagonal

White and black sesame seeds, roasted

A few fresh mint or cilantro leaves (optional)

1. **Short ribs.** Unwrap the short ribs and let sit at room temperature on a wire rack for 30 minutes.

2. Preheat the oven to 250°F (125°C).

3. Season the meat with salt to your taste. In a Dutch oven or other oven-proof heavy, shallow saucepan, over high heat, heat the oil and sear the meat on all sides until nicely browned. Set aside on a plate.

4. **Maple sauce.** In the pot, over high heat, deglaze with the veal stock, scraping the bottom with a wooden spoon to get all the brown bits. Add onions, garlic, ginger, hoisin sauce, oyster sauce, maple syrup, sesame oil and hot pepper sauce to taste, if desired.

5. Return the meat to pot and mix well.

6. Cover and bake for about 5 hours, or until the meat is tender and comes off the bone easily.

7. Stir in raspberries. Bake, uncovered, for 15 minutes or until the fruit is lightly stewed.

8. **For serving.** Cook the rice noodles according to the package directions; drain well. On each plate, place the short ribs on the rice noodles and drizzle with maple sauce. Garnish with edamame, green onions and sesame seeds. If desired, add a few fresh mint or cilantro leaves.

Notes

One whole beef plate short rib has four ribs. For this recipe, you need three. Ask your butcher to cut each of the three pieces in half, perpendicular to the bone, to make 6 pieces total.

You can shorten the cooking time by increasing the oven temperature to 300°F (150°C) and baking for about 4 hours in step 6.

BEEF STEW + LARDONS + COOKING IN A PUMPKIN!

Where the stew cubes come from: the neck, shoulder, brisket, blade, chuck and hind cuts

Serves
4 regular eaters or 2 aggressive eaters
Prep time – 45 min
Cooking time – 3 hours 30 min

2 lbs (1 kg) beef stew cubes

Salt

¼ cup (60 mL) all-purpose flour

7 oz (200 g) lardons or thick bacon,
  cut in matchsticks

2 cups (500 mL) veal stock

1 cup (250 mL) beef stock

1 tbsp (15 mL) pure maple syrup or honey

2 large onions, diced

3 carrots, cut into thick slices

2 stalks celery, cut into thick slices

3 garlic cloves, shoots removed,
  chopped

1 tsp (5 mL) dried marjoram

1 tsp (5 mL) dried thyme

1 tsp (5 mL) onion powder

1 bay leaf

1 pie pumpkin (see Notes)

1. Unwrap the beef cubes and pat dry with paper towel; place in a bowl. Season with salt to your taste and coat evenly with flour. Set aside.

2. In a large saucepan, over medium-high heat, sauté the lardons until they have released their fat. Set aside on a plate, keeping the fat in the saucepan.

3. Sear the beef cubes in this fat until browned. Add the lardons to finish browning them.

4. Deglaze with the veal stock, scraping the bottom with a wooden spoon to get all the brown bits.

5. Stir in beef stock, maple syrup, onions, carrots, celery, garlic, marjoram, thyme, onion powder and bay leaf and bring to a simmer. Reduce the heat to low and simmer, uncovered, for about 2 hours or until the meat is fork tender. Stir two or three times, scraping the bottom of the saucepan during cooking.

6. Meanwhile, cut off the top of the pumpkin and scrape out the insides. Place the pumpkin on a rimmed baking sheet or in roasting pan. If the pumpkin is not stable, cut off a thin slice on the bottom to level it, without making a hole.

7. Preheat the oven to 350°F (180°C).

8. Transfer the stew into the pumpkin. Place in the oven on the lower rack and bake for 1 hour or until the pumpkin is tender. Discard bay leaf.

9. Serve pumpkin on a board or platter in the middle of the table, WITCH is perfect for some Halloween décor. BOO!

Notes

Choose a medium or large pumpkin, but make sure it will fit in
your oven on the lower rack.

For a thicker stew, you can
thicken the sauce further at the
end of step 5, using the technique
given in the note on page 42.

Note

Once the cheeks are cooked, you can strain the cooking liquid and thicken it. Pour the liquid into a small saucepan and bring to a simmer over medium heat. Whisk 2 tablespoons (30 mL) all-purpose flour and 1/4 cup (60 mL) cornstarch with cold water to make a slurry. Pour the mixture into simmering liquid, adding just enough to thicken it to the consistency you want! You may not use all the slurry. Boil until the raw flour taste is cooked out.

BEEF CHEEKS + WINE + MASHED POTATOES + PICKLED SHALLOTS

Where the cheeks come from: the head

Serves
6 reasonable people or
4 unreasonable ones
Prep time – 40 min
Cooking time – 4 hours 30 min

Pickled shallots

¼ cup (60 mL) apple cider vinegar
1 tbsp (15 mL) granulated sugar
½ tsp (2 mL) salt
2 shallots, thinly sliced

Beef cheeks with red wine

Salt
4 beef cheeks
2 tbsp (30 mL) vegetable oil
2 large onions, quartered
3 carrots, peeled and quartered
8 cups (2 L) dry red wine
3 garlic cloves, shoots removed, crushed
3 sprigs of fresh thyme
2 bay leaves
Coarsely ground black pepper to taste

Mashed potatoes

3 large potatoes, peeled and cut into sixths
1 cup (250 mL) hot milk
¼ cup (60 mL) cold salted butter, diced
Salt to taste

For serving (optional)

Snipped fresh chives

1. **Pickled shallots.** In a jar or non-reactive container with a lid, combine vinegar, sugar and salt, stirring until dissolved. Add shallots. Cover and refrigerate for up to 2 weeks.

2. **Beef cheeks with red wine.** Preheat the oven to 300°F (150°C).

3. Season the meat with salt to your taste. In a Dutch oven or other oven-proof heavy, shallow saucepan, over high heat, heat the oil and brown the beef cheeks, turning until browned on all sides. Set aside on a plate.

4. Add onions and carrots to the pot and sauté for 5 to 10 minutes until softened and browned.

5. Return the beef to the pot; stir in wine, garlic, thyme, bay leaves and season with pepper to your taste. Bring to a boil; boil until liquid is reduced by one quarter, skimming any foam that rises to the top to keep the liquid clear.

6. Cover and bake for about 4 hours or until the beef is fork tender.

7. **Mashed potatoes.** In a saucepan, cover the potatoes with water and bring to a boil. Reduce the heat and boil gently for 20 to 30 minutes or until tender. Drain, return to the pot and mash with a masher, or press through a ricer back into the pot. Gradually add the hot milk alternately with the cold butter, mashing or stirring, to blend all the ingredients well. Season with salt to taste. If desired, pass the potatoes through a mesh sieve for a creamier texture.

8. Place some mashed potatoes in the middle of each plate, add one beef cheek and pour a little of the cooking juices (see Note) over it. Garnish with pickled shallots and, if desired, snipped chives.

POT ROAST + GARLIC +
NO DIRTY PANS!

Where the boneless blade chuck roast comes from: the blade

A real treat, which can be served with potatoes and root vegetables!
This roast releases such a comforting aroma during cooking that
they should make it a scent for a candle!

Serves
4 regular eaters
or 2 to 3 competitive eaters
Prep time – 10 min
Tempering – 30 min
Cooking time – 5 hours

1 beef boneless blade chuck roast
(boneless bottom blade pot roast),
about 3 lbs (1.5 kg)

3 tbsp (45 mL) Dijon mustard

4 garlic cloves, shoots removed,
chopped

1 tbsp (15 mL) soy sauce

1 tsp (5 mL) Worcestershire sauce

2 tsp (10 mL) herbes de Provence

Salt and pepper to taste

1 sprig of thyme (optional)

1. Unwrap the roast and let sit at room temperature on a wire rack for 30 minutes.
2. Preheat the oven to 300°F (150°C).
3. In a bowl, combine Dijon mustard, garlic, soy sauce, Worcestershire sauce, herbes de Provence and salt and pepper to your taste.
4. Place a large sheet of foil on a baking sheet; place the roast in the center of the foil and baste with the seasoning mixture. Add the sprig of thyme, if desired.
5. Close up the foil to make a pouch. Cover with a second layer of foil to seal the roast as tightly as possible.
6. Slide the foil pouch off the baking sheet into the oven and bake for 5 hours or until the meat shreds easily with a fork. Slide the pouch back onto the baking sheet to remove it from the oven.
7. Shred the beef or cut across the grain into slices. Serve with any juices from the foil.

Note
You can sear the meat in oil in a hot skillet over high heat before seasoning it and cooking it in the pouch.

FLAT IRON STEAK +
MISO SHALLOTS +
GARLIC AND LEMON YOGURT

Where the flat iron comes from: the blade

Serves
4 calm eaters or 2 excited eaters
Prep time – 45 min
Tempering – 30 min
Cooking time – 25 min
Resting time – 10 min

Steak

1¾ lbs (875 g) beef flat iron steak
 (top blade flat iron steak) (one or
 two pieces)
Salt
2 tbsp (30 mL) vegetable oil

Garlic and lemon yogurt

2 cups (500 mL) plain yogurt
1 tsp (5 mL) lemon zest
2 tbsp (30 mL) lemon juice
2 garlic cloves, shoots removed,
 chopped
Salt and pepper

Miso shallots

¼ cup (60 mL) butter
6 to 8 shallots, cut in half lengthwise
3 tbsp (45 mL) honey
3 tbsp (45 mL) white miso

For serving (optional)

Fresh herbs or microgreens
 (your choice)
A drizzle of honey
A pinch of fleur de sel

1. Steak. Unwrap the steak and let sit at room temperature on a wire rack for 30 minutes.

2. Garlic and lemon yogurt. Combine yogurt, lemon zest and juice and garlic in a bowl; season with salt and pepper to taste. Cover and refrigerate.

3. Miso shallots. In a skillet, over medium-high heat, melt the butter. Place the shallots flat side down. Cook without stirring until the butter foams and the shallots are nicely browned. Add the honey and miso. Flip the shallots and baste them with the honey miso butter using a spoon. Remove from the heat.

4. Season the meat with salt to your taste. In another skillet, over high heat, heat the oil and sear the steak until nicely browned, turning it over halfway through cooking (recommended internal temperature of between 125 and 131°F/52 and 55°C; see page 18). Set aside on a plate and let rest for about 10 minutes.

5. Spread a few spoonfuls of garlic and lemon yogurt on each plate. Add the shallots and some of their juice. Slice the steak across the grain and spread the slices on the plates. If desired, garnish with fresh herbs or microgreens. Finish with a drizzle of honey and a pinch of fleur de sel.

Note

To cook the steak on the grill, preheat the barbecue to high for a gas grill or use a charcoal chimney starter to get glowing coals on a charcoal barbecue. Sear the steak over direct heat on the grill or on the coals.

1 beef tomahawk steak, about 3 lbs
(1.5 kg)
Salt

Chunky mashed potatoes

3 large potatoes, peeled and cut in
1-inch (2.5 cm) slices
3 tbsp (45 mL) vegetable oil
Salt and pepper to taste
$\frac{1}{2}$ lb (250 g) lardons or thick-cut
bacon cut into matchsticks
2 garlic cloves, shoots removed,
chopped finely
2 onions, diced
2 tbsp (30 mL) butter

TOMAHAWK + COALS + POTATOES + LARDONS

Where the tomahawk comes from: the rib

A perfect recipe for true carnivores who love having fun with coals!
The mashed potatoes are not a minor character: the judges on the *La Coupe BBQ*
LOVED them during the first round of the competition!

Serves – 5 little birds or 3 pigs
Prep time – 30 min   **Tempering** – 45 min   **Cooking time** – 1 hour   **Resting time** – 15 min

1. Tomahawk. Unwrap the tomahawk and let sit at room temperature on a wire rack for 45 minutes.

2. Use a charcoal chimney starter to get nicely burning coals and place it on one side of the barbecue.

3. Chunky mashed potatoes. In a bowl, combine the potatoes with the oil. Add salt and pepper to taste. Grill the potatoes over direct heat until nicely browned. Turn over to brown the other side. Move the slices to continue cooking over indirect heat until potatoes are tender.

4. Place a cast-iron skillet on the grill over direct heat. Add lardons, garlic and onions. Cook until golden brown while stirring.

5. Place the cooked potatoes in the cast-iron skillet and mash them coarsely with a fork to get a chunky mash. Stir well to coat the potatoes with the lardons mixture. Add the butter and let foam until you get brown butter. Stir and add salt and pepper to taste.

Remove from the heat and set aside in the skillet (the potatoes will be reheated while the meat is resting).

6. Season the steak with salt to your taste and place it directly on the coals. Turn it to sear it on all sides. If pieces of charcoal stick to the meat, remove them with tongs.

7. Remove the steak from the coals, place it on the barbecue grill and continue cooking over indirect heat. Cook to an internal temperature of 125 to 130°F (52 to 54°C); see page 18. Set aside on a plate and let rest for about 15 minutes (meanwhile, reheat the potatoes over direct heat on the grill).

8. Cut the steak into pieces, muscle by muscle (see page 27) or in slices.

9. To serve, place the mashed potatoes in the middle of a large wood plank. Place the pieces of steak on top, as well as the bone for decoration. Set the plank in the center of the table and share!

BEEF

HINDQUARTER BEEF CUTS

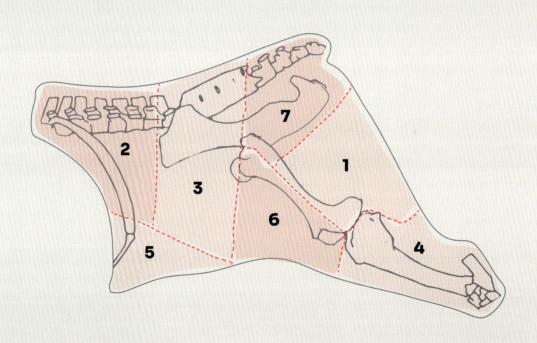

1 – ROUND
2 – LOIN
3 – SIRLOIN
4 – SHANK (HIND)

5 – FLANK
6 – SIRLOIN TIP
7 – RUMP

1 – THE ROUND

This is a part of the cow's thigh. It contains the top (inside) round, outside round (bottom round) and eye of round. Generally speaking, the round is much less tender and less expensive than tenderloin but has a lot more flavor. When it is not mechanically tenderized, it can be used raw, such as in steak tartare. A whole top (inside) round, which has a round shape, is covered by the inside round cap, and hides a cluster of meat where you will find the bullet muscle (gracilis) or petite poire (meaning "little pear" in French), a delicious and tender muscle whose shape and size resemble that of a pear. When the inside round cap, the cluster of meat, bullet muscle and fat are removed (this is called "complete trim"), you get a boneless top (inside) round. One muscle found here is called the adductor muscle. The adductor can easily be removed because of its natural separation; you can recognize it by the small blood vessel that runs through rhe muscle. The adductor is often used for roasts and steaks, but also for tartare. Deboned top (inside) round muscles offer lean, tasty and economical pieces. It is often tenderized mechanically to make steaks, roasts, kabob cubes, strips and beef tournedos or medallions. Prepared as a roast that is not mechanically tenderized, it can also be delicious cooked blue or rare (see page 18) and sliced thinly across the grain. For this cut, we want to keep the meat juicy and tender, so cooking longer than to medium-rare doneness is not recommended.

Eye of round is a lean muscle that is often used to make thin slices for hot pot or Chinese fondue (because of its round shape). It can also be prepared as a roast, as tournedos (tenderized or not) as well as cubes to grill or simmer.

Finally, the bottom (outside) round is rather tough. It is often mechanically tenderized to make cubes for cube steak or minute steak.

For connoisseurs: In the round, near the bullet muscle, there's a small muscle worth grilling, called the pectineus or merlan.

Important note: You need to make sure that inside round has not been mechanically tenderized before making a tartare or a tataki. Mechanically tenderized meats must always be cooked to a minimum internal temperature of 145°F (63 °C) to avoid possible contamination caused by bacteria being transferred to the center of the meat that was pricked by the tenderizer.

WHOLESALE CUT: ROUND	
Retail cut	**Cooking method**
Sandwich steak	Grill, sauté
Round steak (tenderized), French steak, tournedos/medallions	Grill, sauté
Eye of round, top (inside) round, bullet muscle as carpaccio	Raw
Kabob cubes (cubes, tenderized or not)	Grill
Lean stew cubes	Braise, simmer
Fast-fry steaks, cutlets	Grill, sauté
Eye of round (thin slices for hot pot/Chinese fondue)	Simmer, sauté

WHOLESALE CUT: ROUND	
Retail cut	**Cooking method**
Top (inside) round sub-primal	Raw (not tenderized), grill, sauté
- *individual muscle: inside round cap* (for lean stew cubes)	*Braise, simmer*
- *Individual muscle: adductor*	*Raw, fry, grill, sauté*
- *Individual muscle: pectineus (merlan)*	*Raw, grill, sauté*
- *Individual muscle: bullet (gracilis)*	*Raw, fry, grill, sauté*
Strips (tenderized or not)	Grill, sauté
Denuded top (inside) round (thin slices for stuffed rolls, e.g. rosettes, roulades, or involtini)	Grill, sauté
Top (inside) round roast, tenderized or not	Roast
Bullet muscle, denuded top (inside) round as tartare	Raw

2 – THE LOIN

This is one of the wholesale cuts that includes muscles that the animal uses less. Here, we also find a part of the tenderloin (also called the filet), the most tender muscle of the carcass but one that doesn't have much flavor. There is also the strip (strip loin). The loin primal is made up of vertebrae, feather bones and transverse processes. When the sub-primal short loin is sliced crosswise, you get a T-bone steak: the tenderloin (or filet) and the strip (strip loin) are separated in the middle by bones that form a T (see page 53). The slices from the sirloin end of the short loin, closer to the tenderloin head (butt) (see For connoisseurs, below), are called "porterhouse," while the slices (with the rib bone) toward the rib primal, with a small or no tenderloin (filet), are called bone-in strip steak.

For connoisseurs: The whole tenderloin includes five sections: the head (also called the butt, and found in the sirloin), the center, the heart (which is the fleshy, even part of the center), the tail and the chain, a muscle that runs along the tenderloin. The head (butt), which is wider, contains a group of muscles. The tail is much narrower. So, the loin includes a large filet part (closer to the porterhouse section toward the sirloin primal) and a small filet part (closer to the rib primal).

WHOLESALE CUT: LOIN	
Retail cut	**Cooking method**
T-bone and Porterhouse steak	Grill, sauté
Strip steak (strip loin steak)	Raw, grill, sauté
Bone-in strip steak	Grill, sauté
Strip roast (strip loin roast, bone-in or boneless)	Roast
Tenderloin steak (filet mignon)	Raw, grill, sauté
Wing steak	Grill, sauté
Whole tenderloin	Raw, grill, sauté
- *individual muscle: chain (one part)*	*Grill, sauté*
Bone-in tenderloin, steak or roast	Grill (steaks), roast
Wing rib roast	Roast

STRIP (STRIP LOIN)

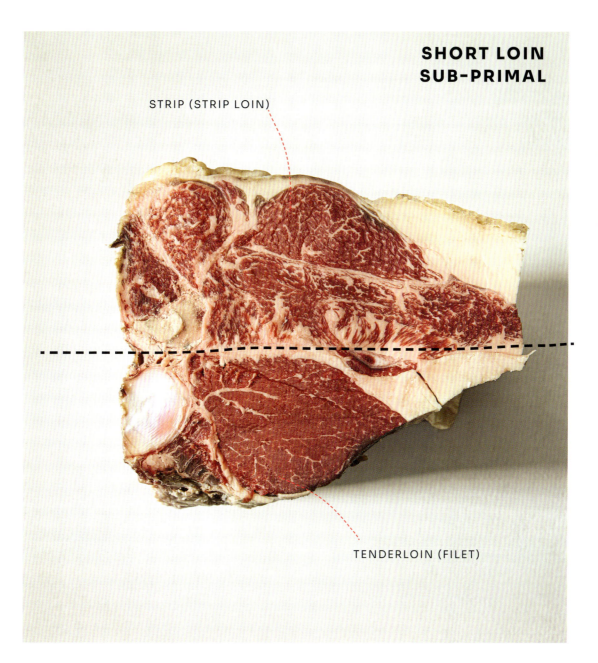

TENDERLOIN (FILET)

3 – THE SIRLOIN

Sirloin, which translates from the French "surlonge" to "above the loin," contains two interesting lean and flavorful parts: the top sirloin butt (see photo) and the bottom sirloin butt. The top sirloin contains the steak part, the top sirloin butt, center-cut (also known as the top sirloin heart or top sirloin cap off/removed) and the coulotte, a triangular meat cut with a layer of fat on the surface. Often called the picanha (a Brazilian word), it is delicious grilled, either whole or as a steak. The top sirloin butt, center-cut (also called cœur de Boston in Quebec) is a very tender muscle. When sliced, it is often known as baseball steak, because its shape is like . . . a baseball! This cut can also be delicious for roasts. The bottom sirloin contains the head (butt) of the tenderloin, a small part of the bavette and the tri-tip (bottom sirloin tri-tip), an excellent piece to grill. Today, the bavette and the tenderloin are increasingly removed whole from the carcass, given their popularity.

For connoisseurs: If you want a muscle that will melt in your MOUSE, the mouse muscle (which in French is actually called the langue de chat. This means cat tongue and it's called that because the cut does resemble a cat's tongue.) is a small, tasty and extremely tender muscle found under the top sirloin butt. Grilled or raw, it's the cat's meow!

WHOLESALE CUT: SIRLOIN	
Retail cut	**Cooking method**
Sirloin bavette steak (bottom sirloin flap steak)	Raw, grill, sauté
Sirloin steak (whole) - *individual muscle: fausse araignée (false spider)* - *individual muscle: mouse* - *individual muscle: oyster or spider (groin)* - *individual muscle: tri-tip*	Grill, roast (if sliced thickly) *Simmer* *Raw, grill, sauté* *Grill, sauté* *Raw, grill, roast, sauté*
Top sirloin steak, boneless (top sirloin steak)	Raw (if trimmed of fat), grill, sauté
Whole sirloin steak, bone-in (without filet)	Grill, roast (if sliced thickly)
Top sirloin butt, center-cut (steak or roast)	Grill, roast, sauté
Stew cubes	Braise, simmer
Coulotte/picanha (whole)	Raw (if trimmed of fat), grill, roast
Coulotte/picanha (sliced)	Grill, sauté
Tenderloin head (butt) steaks	Grill, sauté
Fondue Bourguignon	Fry, sauté
Top sirloin medallions	Raw, grill, sauté
Top sirloin roast, boneless	Roast
Tenderloin head (butt) roast	Grill, roast
Tenderloin medallions wrapped with lard (tournedos)	Grill, sauté

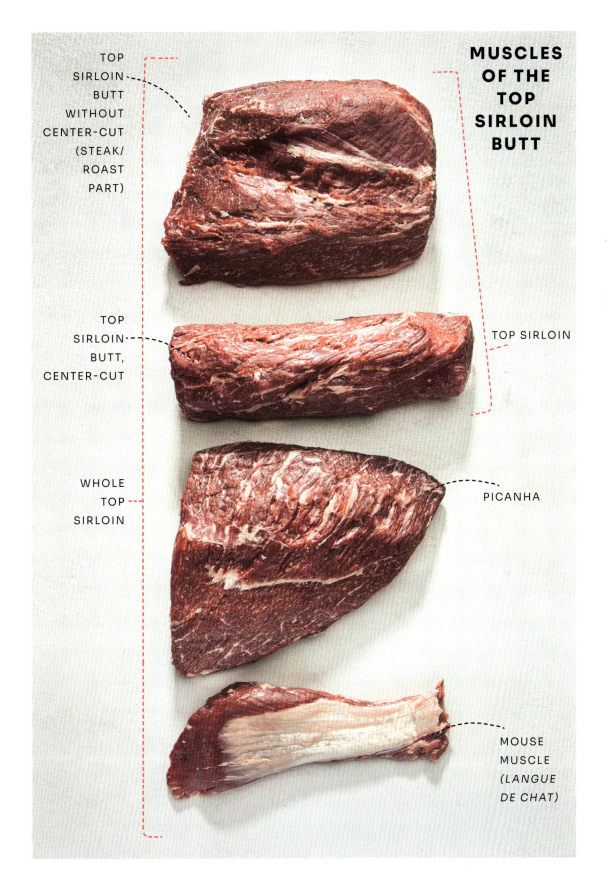

TOP SIRLOIN BUTT WITHOUT CENTER-CUT (STEAK/ROAST PART)

TOP SIRLOIN BUTT, CENTER-CUT

WHOLE TOP SIRLOIN

MUSCLES OF THE TOP SIRLOIN BUTT

TOP SIRLOIN

PICANHA

MOUSE MUSCLE (*LANGUE DE CHAT*)

4 – THE SHANK (HIND)

The hindshank includes the tibia bone, which contains marrow, and is meatier than the foreshank. Also, several small muscles that surround it have a good amount of collagen. These characteristics make it an excellent choice for braised dishes, stews and fall soups. It becomes tender after being cooked for a long time at a low temperature; it also lends itself to cooking in the smoker and on the barbecue in summertime. Grilling or frying a beef shank is not recommended; doing so could cost you a fortune at the dentist because it will be tough! The shank can be found in various forms: boneless, sliced, whole and even with the meat trimmed off the ends of the long bone, known as Thor's hammer.

WHOLESALE CUT: SHANK (HIND)	
Retail cut	**Cooking method**
Shank center-cut (sliced or whole)	Braise, simmer
Boneless shank	Braise, simmer
Thor's hammer (Frenched shank)	Braise, simmer

5 – THE FLANK

The flank primal contains part of the sirloin bavette (bottom sirloin flap) and the flank steak. The flank steak is much less tender than the bavette, as it contains long, thick muscle fibers. This dense texture makes this cut less enjoyable to chew. However, flank steak is wonderful in stews, as a stuffed cutlet or roast and it's a popular choice for marinating and grilling. Part of the skirt steak, the inside skirt, is also found in the flank; it's marbled and very flavorful. This muscle is similar to the bavette, although much narrower and not as thick. What sets the flank apart is the robust flavor of the cuts made from it.

WHOLESALE CUT: FLANK	
Retail cut	**Cooking method**
Bavette (extension of the sirloin)	Raw, grill, sauté
Flank steak	Grill, simmer
Flank, stuffed and rolled	Braise, grill, simmer, roast
Skirt (inside)	Raw, grill, sauté

WHOLE SIRLOIN TIP SUB-PRIMAL

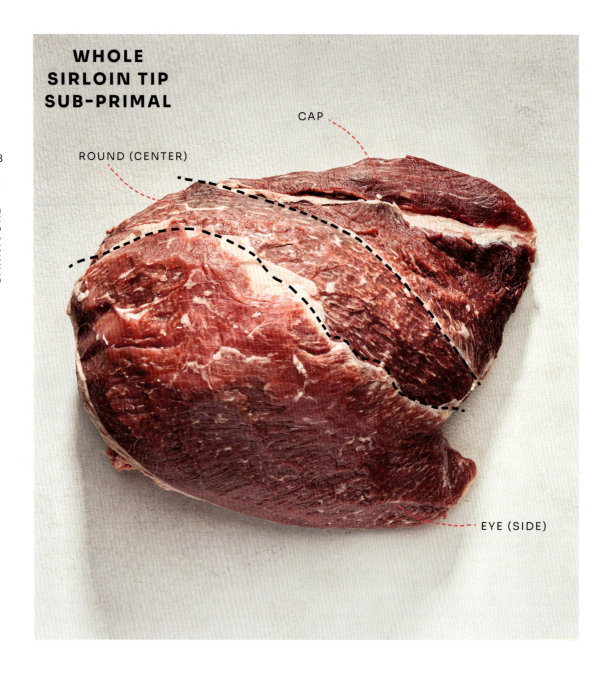

CAP

ROUND (CENTER)

EYE (SIDE)

6 – THE SIRLOIN TIP

The sirloin tip may also be called the knuckle. It contains three main parts: the round (center), the eye (side) and the cap. The round is the most tender part of the sirloin tip and is often used for roasts, grilling cuts and kabob cubes. It contains a central nerve that can be removed to separate the two muscles. The eye is much less tender. It is often (but not always) mechanically tenderized to make roasts, steaks and kabob cubes. It can also be prepared as fast-fry steaks or cutlets. Part of the cap can be made into stew cubes or fast-fry steaks or cutlets, while the rest is often ground, given its lack of tenderness.

WHOLESALE CUT: SIRLOIN TIP	
Retail cut	**Cooking method**
Sandwich Steak	Grill, sauté
Cube steak/minute steak (mechanically tenderized)	Grill, sauté
Sirloin tip steak	Grill, sauté
Kabob cubes	Grill, sauté
Stew cubes (cap)	Braise, simmer
Fast-fry steaks/cutlets/scaloppini (eye)	Grill, sauté
Beef for hot pot (Chinese fondue)	Simmer, sauté
Sirloin tip roast (round)	Roast
Sirloin tip eye (side) roast (mechanically tenderized)	Roast

7 – THE RUMP

This sub-primal cut is part of the hip (included in the round primal cut); it is separated by a clean cut that is more or less parallel to and close to the aitch bone. It is divided into two parts: the inside and outside rump. The inside rump, which is more tender, can be roasted, although it is more and more common to find it mechanically tenderized. Today, the rump is increasingly hard to find, as it is kept with the round.

WHOLESALE CUT: RUMP	
Retail cut	**Cooking method**
Cube steak/minute steak (mechanically tenderized)	Grill, sauté
Lean stew cubes	Braise, simmer
Boneless rump roast	Roast
Outside rump roast (bone in)	Roast
Inside rump roast (bone in)	Roast

FILET MIGNON + BONE MARROW + ESCARGOTS + ARUGULA PESTO

Where filet mignon comes from: the loin or the sirloin (the tenderloin head/butt)

Serves
2 moderate people
or 1 very determined person
Prep time – 30 min
Tempering – 30 min
Cooking time – 20 min
Resting time – 10 min

Filets mignons

2 filets mignon steaks (tenderloin steaks), 10 oz (300 g) each

2 cross-cut slices bone marrow, about ½ inch (1 cm) thick

Salt

Arugula pesto

1 ¼ cups (310 mL) arugula

1 cup (250 mL) fresh parsley leaves and tender stems

½ cup (125 mL) cashews (or your choice of nuts)

¼ cup (25 g) grated Parmesan

¼ cup (60 mL) extra virgin olive oil (approx.)

Fried escargots

2 tbsp (30 mL) vegetable oil

¼ cup (60 mL) butter

1 can (4 oz/115 g) escargots, rinsed and drained

3 garlic cloves, shoots removed, finely chopped

1 shallot, finely chopped

Fresh parsley, chopped finely, to taste

For serving

Shaved Parmesan

Lemon zest

Equipment

Butcher's twine

1. Filets mignons. Unwrap the steaks and let sit at room temperature on a wire rack for 30 minutes.

2. Arugula pesto. In a food processor, purée arugula, parsley, cashews and Parmesan until finely chopped. Drizzle in enough of the olive oil until you get a smooth and creamy texture. Cover and refrigerate.

3. Preheat the barbecue to high on just one side of the grill; for a charcoal grill, use a charcoal chimney starter to get glowing coals and place it at one end of the grill.

4. Place a slice of bone marrow on each steak. Tie together with twine, making a bow on top (like a present!).

5. Evenly salt the meat to your taste. Sear on the grill over direct heat or place directly on the coals. Cook until the steaks are nicely browned on all sides, turning them halfway through cooking. If pieces of charcoal stick to the meat, remove them with tongs.

6. Continue cooking over indirect heat (if over charcoal, add the barbecue rack back in), bone marrow side up, until the internal temperature reaches 120°F (50°C) for rare (see page 18) or to your desired doneness. Set aside on a plate and let rest for 10 minutes.

7. Fried escargots. Place a cast-iron skillet on the barbecue over direct heat. Heat oil and melt butter. Add escargots, garlic and shallot. Sauté for about 10 minutes or until escargots are sizzling hot. Add chopped parsley, stir and set aside.

8. Spread some pesto onto individual serving plates. Place a steak with the marrow slice up on each plate. Garnish with escargots. Decorate with a few curls of Parmesan and lemon zest.

Note
You can also cook this recipe on the stove, using a grill pan or cast-iron skillet for the steaks.

PICANHA + CHIMICHURRI + TOMATO + ONION

Where the picanha comes from: the sirloin

A remix of Argentinian chimichurri and Mexican pico de gallo: perfect for pairing with Brazilian picanha!

Serves
4 to 6 reasonable eaters or
3 aggressive eaters
Prep time – 25 min
Tempering – 30 min
Cooking time – 50 min
Resting time – 10 to 15 min

Picanha

1 whole picanha, about 3 lbs (1.5 kg)
Salt

Tomato and onion chimichurri

1½ cups (375 mL) vegetable oil
Zest of 1 lime
Juice of 2 limes
¼ cup (60 mL) chopped fresh oregano
¼ cup (60 mL) chopped fresh cilantro
1 cup (250 mL) diced seeded tomatoes
¼ cup (60 mL) diced white onion
Chopped jalapeño

1. **Picanha.** If desired, trim the fat from the roast to your taste and remove the membrane on the meat side. Let sit at room temperature on a wire rack for 30 minutes.

2. **Tomato and onion chimichurri.** In a large bowl, combine oil, lime zest, lime juice, oregano, cilantro, tomatoes and onion. Stir in jalapeño to taste. Refrigerate.

3. Preheat the barbecue to high on just one side of a gas grill; for a charcoal grill, use a charcoal chimney starter to get glowing coals and place it at one end of the grill.

4. Evenly salt the meat to your taste. Place it on the grill over direct heat or directly on the coals. Sear the picanha on all sides until nicely browned, turning it over halfway through cooking. If pieces of charcoal stick to the meat, remove them with tongs.

5. On a gas grill, move roast to the unlit side of grill. If cooking on the coals, return the grill to the barbecue and place roast on the grill. Adjust the heat to 275°F (135°C) ideally, or up to 350°F (180°C) and cook over indirect heat.

6. Insert a heat-safe thermometer into the center of the meat and cook for about 45 minutes, or until the internal temperature reaches 127°F (53°C) for very rare, or to desired doneness.

7. Set on a wire rack and let rest for 10 to 15 minutes.

8. Slice the roast across the grain. Serve with the tomato and onion chimichurri.

Note

The picanha roast may also be called a coulotte roast or top sirloin cap roast.

BAVETTE + SWEET POTATOES + SOUR CREAM + LIME + CILANTRO

Where bavette comes from: the flank and the sirloin

I love to serve this simple summer recipe in tacos, too.

Serves
2 to 3 fit eaters or
1 Olympic eater
Prep time – 45 min
Tempering – 20 min
Cooking time – 1 hour
Resting time – 5 to 10 min

2 medium sweet potatoes

1 piece of beef sirloin bavette/flap
 (bottom sirloin bavette), about
 1⅓ lbs (600 g)

1½ cups (375 mL) sour cream

¼ cup (60 mL) fresh cilantro leaves

Zest and juice of 1 lime

2 tbsp (30 mL) onion powder

1 garlic clove, shoot removed, chopped

Ground cumin

Chopped jalapeño

Salt to taste

1. Preheat the barbecue to high on just one side of the grill; for a charcoal grill, use a charcoal chimney starter to get glowing coals and place it at one end of the grill.

2. Scrub the sweet potatoes. Prick them all over with a knife or fork. Wrap each potato in foil and place them on the grill over direct heat or in the coals. Turn often to brown each side (check by carefully opening the foil). Re-wrap and continue cooking over indirect heat for about 20 minutes or until sweet potatoes are tender.

3. Unwrap the beef and let sit at room temperature on a wire rack for 20 minutes.

4. In a food processor or blender, blend sour cream, cilantro, lime zest and juice, onion powder, garlic and cumin and jalapeño to your taste until smooth. Refrigerate.

5. Evenly salt the beef to your taste. Place on the grill over direct heat or in the coals. Cook until the meat is nicely browned on all sides, turning it over half-way through cooking. If pieces of charcoal stick to the meat, remove them with tongs. Continue cooking over indirect heat, if needed, until the internal temperature reaches 131°F (55°C) for very rare (see page 18) or to desired doneness.

6. Set aside on a plate and let rest for 5 to 10 minutes.

7. Slice the meat across the grain. Serve with the sweet potatoes and the cilantro-lime sour cream.

FLANK STEAK +
STROGANOFF

Where flank steak comes from: the flank

Serves
4 little mice or 2 wolves
Prep time – 25 min
Tempering – 20 min
Cooking time – 2 hours 10 min

1 beef flank steak, about 2¼ lbs (1 kg)
¼ cup (60 mL) all-purpose flour
Salt and pepper
¼ cup (60 mL) vegetable oil
2 tbsp (30 mL) butter
4 garlic cloves, shoots removed, chopped
3 onions, chopped
2 lbs (908 g) button mushrooms
1 cup (250 mL) red wine
1½ cups (375 mL) veal stock
2 tbsp (30 mL) Dijon mustard
1 tsp (5 mL) paprika
1¼ cups (310 mL) sour cream
Fresh flat-leaf parsley, chopped finely, to taste (optional)

1. Unwrap the steak and let sit at room temperature on a wire rack for 20 minutes.
2. Cut the steak across the grain into strips about ¾ inch (2 cm) thick. In a bowl, sprinkle the beef strips with flour, then salt and pepper to your taste, tossing to coat.
3. In a skillet, over high heat, heat the oil and sauté the strips, in batches as necessary, until golden and crispy. Set aside on a plate.
4. In the same skillet, melt butter and sauté garlic, onions and mushrooms.
5. Deglaze with red wine, scraping the bottom with a wooden spoon to get all the brown bits. Add the reserved steak strips, veal stock, Dijon mustard and paprika. Stir well.
6. Cover and simmer over low heat, stirring occasionally, for about 2 hours or until the meat is tender.
7. Add sour cream, stir and reheat without boiling.
8. Garnish with parsley, if desired, and serve.

Note
To decorate, I like making carrot disks that I fry in a skillet with butter. I make four small holes with a toothpick and insert sprigs of chive before cooking. These make pretty little carrot buttons!

Note

If the oil isn't cold enough, the pearls won't solidify. If this happens to you, put the oil back in the freezer and reheat the caper brine mixture just before making the pearls.

Caper pearls

2 cups (500 mL) vegetable oil

⅓ cup (80 mL) caper brine
(the liquid from a jar of capers)

½ tsp (2 mL) agar–agar

Caesar tartar sauce

1 egg yolk

1 tbsp (15 mL) freshly squeezed
lemon juice

2 garlic cloves, shoots removed,
finely chopped

2 tbsp (30 mL) chopped capers

1 tbsp (15 mL) anchovy paste

¾ cup (175 mL) vegetable oil

½ cup (45 g) freshly grated
Parmesan

Salt and pepper

Parmesan crisps

¼ cup (25 g) freshly grated Parmesan

Tartare

14 oz (400 g) beef top (inside) round
steak or roast, not tenderized, cut
into very small cubes

1 romaine lettuce leaf, finely
chopped

2 slices cooked bacon, coarsely
crumbled

Salt and pepper

Equipment

1 eyedropper
(available at pharmacies)

TARTARE + CAESAR + CAPER PEARLS + PARMESAN CRISPS

Where top (inside) round comes from: the round

Serves – 2 calm people or 1 energetic person
Prep time – 25 min   **Freezer time** – 30 to 45 min   **Cooking time** – 10 min   **Resting time** – 5 to 10 min

1. Caper pearls. Pour the oil for the caper pearls into a tall container, like a juice glass. Place in the freezer for 30 to 45 minutes before mixing. Put a large bowl in the fridge.
2. Preheat the oven to 375°F (190°C). Line a baking sheet with parchment paper.
3. Caesar tartar sauce. In a bowl, combine egg yolk, lemon juice, garlic, capers and anchovy paste. Drizzle in oil, while whisking constantly, to whip the sauce like a mayonnaise. Add Parmesan and stir. Add salt and pepper to taste. Cover and refrigerate.
4. In a small saucepan, over high heat, bring to a boil the caper brine and agar-agar. Remove from the heat and fill the eyedropper with hot liquid.
5. Remove oil from the freezer. One drop at a time, add caper brine mixture to the oil; the pearls will solidify when they come into contact with the oil (see Note). Turn all the liquid into caper pearls in this way.

6. Strain oil with a sieve to keep only the pearls. Immerse the pearls in a bowl of cold water to remove excess oil. Strain again and store the pearls in the fridge. Discard the oil.
7. Parmesan crisps. Spread Parmesan in a thin, even layer on the prepared pan. Bake for about 7 minutes, or until the cheese is golden. Let rest for 5 to 10 minutes. With your hands, break pieces of Parmesan to your desired size for presentation.
8. Tartare. In the chilled bowl, combine beef, lettuce and bacon; stir in Caesar tartar sauce to taste. Add salt and pepper to taste and toss well.
9. Serve the tartare with a few caper pearls, the Parmesan crisps and the extra Caesar Tartar Sauce on the side, if desired.

ROAST + BEEF
= SANDWICHES

Where top (inside) round roast comes from: the round

This roast beef is delectable, whether it's for a picnic, for lunch, in a sandwich, in a salad or as charcuterie at cocktail hour with mustard and pickles.

Serves
7 armchair athletes or
4 to 5 football players
Prep time – 15 min
Tempering – 30 min
Cooking time – 1 hour 40 min

1 beef top round roast (inside round roast), not tenderized, about 3⅓ lbs (1.5 kg)

12 garlic cloves, shoots removed, cut in half

Salt to taste

3 tbsp (45 mL) vegetable oil

¼ cup (60 mL) Dijon mustard

3 tbsp (45 mL) steak seasoning

Equipment

Butcher's twine (optional)

1. Unwrap the roast and cut off the twine, if necessary. Let sit at room temperature on a wire rack for 30 minutes.

2. Preheat the oven to 275°F (135°C).

3. Using a long knife, make a shallow incision lengthwise along the center of the roast. Insert the garlic cloves one at a time to fill the cavity.

4. Evenly and generously salt the roast over every surface.

5. In a skillet, over medium-high heat, heat oil and sear the roast on all sides until nicely browned. Remove from heat.

6. Baste the roast with mustard and season with the steak seasoning.

7. Place a rack in a shallow roasting pan; set the roast on the rack. Roast for about 1 hour and 30 minutes or until the internal temperature reaches 120°F (50°C) for rare or to desired doneness.

8. Let the roast cool completely in the fridge before slicing it very thinly across the grain.

MELTED BRIE + BEEF + BARBECUE

Perfect for endless cocktail hours on the porch or patio in summertime!
All you need is some good bread to dip in this decadent dish.

Serves
2 people as a main course or
4 people as an appetizer
Prep time – 10 min
Cooking time – 20 min

1 small wheel Brie cheese (about 7 oz/200 g)

7 oz (200 g) thinly sliced beef for hot pot (Chinese fondue)

2 tbsp (30 mL) vegetable oil

1 lb (450 g) button mushrooms, sliced

1 red bell pepper, cut in strips

1 large onion, sliced

3 tbsp (45 mL) salted butter

2 garlic cloves, shoots removed, crushed

2 sprigs of fresh thyme

Crusty bread, grilled, if desired

Chopped fresh parsley to taste (optional)

1. Wrap the Brie well with slices of beef (2 to 3 layers). Cover and refrigerate.

2. Preheat the barbecue to high; for a charcoal grill, use a charcoal chimney starter to get glowing coals.

3. Pour oil into a large cast-iron or fire-resistant skillet. Place it on the grill rack to cook over direct heat. Place the wrapped Brie in the center of the skillet.

4. Cook until nicely browned and crusty. Flip the cheese and add mushrooms, red pepper and onion to the skillet, surrounding the cheese.

5. Add butter, garlic and thyme to the vegetables. Let the butter foam, then baste the vegetables and cheese with a spoon. When the butter is brown, remove the skillet from heat.

6. Serve in the skillet with bread. If desired, garnish with parsley for a fresh touch.

Notes

Look for very thin slices of beef ribeye, top sirloin or flank steak for Asian hot pots or Chinese fondue. They are sometimes packaged as rolls of beef.

If needed, move the Brie to indirect heat and keep cooking until the center is runny. You can also sear the Brie in a skillet on the stove and continue cooking in a 375°F (190°C) oven for 10 to 15 minutes, or until the Brie is melted.

THOR'S HAMMER +
SWEET MOP SAUCE + CANDLE

Where Thor's hammer comes from: the shank (fore or hind)

Serves – 6 peaceful eaters or 4 not-so-peaceful eaters
Prep time – 1 hour   **Refrigeration** – 12 hours   **Tempering** – 1 hour
Cooking time – about 5 hours   **Resting time** – 30 min

Flavor infusion

6 oz (180 g) beef suet (see Note, page 36)
¼ cup (60 mL) beef stock
1½ tsp (7 mL) Worcestershire sauce
1 can (5½ oz/156 mL) seasoned vegetable cocktail
1 tsp (5 mL) soy sauce
1 tsp (5 mL) onion powder
½ tsp (2 mL) ground black pepper

Thor's hammer

1 beef Thor's hammer (whole shank, Frenched/trimmed)
Salt and pepper

Sweet mop sauce

1 cup (250 mL) ketchup
¼ cup (60 mL) prepared yellow mustard
¼ cup (60 mL) light (fancy) molasses
2 tbsp (30 mL) soy sauce
2 tbsp (30 mL) Worcestershire sauce
2 garlic cloves, shoots removed, finely chopped
2 tsp (10 mL) onion powder
¼ cup (60 mL) lager beer (the rest is for quenching your thirst!)

Equipment

1 syringe/injector
Smoking wood chips
1 mop-style dishcloth (or brush)
1 piece of butcher's twine (or wooden skewer), 4 inches (10 cm)
  long
Parchment paper and foil or butcher paper

Directions: see next page

1. Flavor infusion. In a bowl, combine all the ingredients until smooth.

2. Thor's hammer. With the syringe, inject the flavor infusion into the shank in the direction of the meat fibers every 2 inches (5 cm). Wrap in plastic wrap, place in a shallow dish and refrigerate for at least 12 hours or for up to 24 hours.

3. Unwrap the meat and let sit at room temperature on a wire rack for 1 hour.

4. Sweet mop sauce. In a saucepan, over high heat, bring to a boil all the sauce ingredients; reduce heat and simmer for 5 to 10 minutes, stirring occasionally. Set aside.

5. Preheat the smoker or barbecue to between 250 and 300°F (120 and 150°C). If needed, remove the upper rack so you can cook the meat (which is a rather impressive size) on the lower rack. Once the internal temperature of the smoker or the barbecue is reached, add the smoking wood of your choice.

6. Generously season the meat with salt and pepper to your taste. Smoke over indirect heat. After 1 hour of smoking, baste with mop sauce.

7. When the meat reaches an internal temperature of 170°F (77 °C), remove it from the smoker and place it on a large sheet of parchment paper. Baste generously with sauce and close up in a pouch. Cover the entire pouch in foil or butcher paper to preserve optimal humidity.

8. Return the meat to indirect heat and cook until the internal temperature reaches 205 to 210°F (96 to 98°C). If the thermometer does not go into the meat easily like butter (insert it through the pouch), continue cooking until tender. Let the meat rest, wrapped, for 30 minutes before serving.

9. When serving, unwrap and baste with mop sauce. Insert the twine (or skewer) lengthwise down the center of the marrow, leaving 1 inch (2.5 cm) showing at the top of the bone. Place on the center of the table and light the Thor's hammer like a candle!

> **Note**
> Americans are very fond of barbecue, and they often do massive ones that attract huge crowds! For these, they use an actual mop (clean, used only for this purpose) to baste the huge pieces of meat more easily and quickly. Sauces are therefore a bit more liquid, to make the task easier . . . for the mop!

PORK

Despite being a forbidden meat in some religions, pork is the most highly consumed meat in the world and is produced on every continent except Antarctica. Economical and versatile, pork also has a large presence in various processed foods, such as charcuterie. Its gelatinous qualities are used in gummy sweets (jujubes), and the fat (lard), which is inexpensive, is found in all kinds of products, from foods to cosmetics.

Pork is a versatile meat with lots of flavor and plenty of ways to use it because it goes well with many ingredients. With fairly fine meat fibers much like those found in veal, pork is often used in traditional veal recipes in the United States instead, due to its lower cost.

Another great feature of pork is that the entire carcass can be cooked, even the caul fat, a membrane between the stomach and diaphragm that looks like lace (see Notes, page 94). Pork is never eaten raw or rare, though it can safely be eaten slightly pink, especially lean cuts, like the loin — and when overcooked, it is as dry as a soda cracker! Like beef, pork can be tempered.

Pigs are much smaller animals than beef calves and cattle, which is why there are fewer cuts: the muscles are much smaller. In pig farming, there are a number of breeds, in particular Yorkshire, Landrace, Duroc, Large White, Pietrain and Iberian. Economical and incredibly delicious, pork is definitely worth pigging out on!

PORK

CUTS

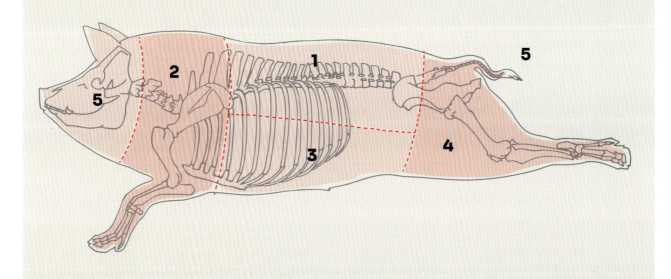

1 – LOIN
2 – SHOULDER
3 – SIDE/BELLY
4 – LEG
5 – HEAD AND TAIL

The loin includes three main parts (see top photo on page 82). First, the loin rib (blade end), which contains the first ribs of the loin. This is the part attached to the shoulder. It is often used for chops or boneless roasts. Next, the loin center-cut, the most highly prized part of this wholesale cut, which contains most of the ribs as well as the tenderloin. The center-cut is used for pork chops and roasts. As a roast, once the meat is removed from the ends of the bones, it becomes a Frenched rib roast (or rack of pork). When all the ribs are removed in one piece, they become a rack of back ribs, commonly called "baby back ribs." The tenderloin side of the loin contains, of course, the pork tenderloin. When the tenderloin is not totally removed, you can make bone-in center-cut chops, equivalent to a T-bone for pork, sometimes called porterhouse chops. Finally, the loin sirloin, as its name indicates, comes from the extension of the sirloin. Often used for roasts, chops and even kabob cubes, it's sometimes called "buckeye." It is versatile and inexpensive.

For connoisseurs: A small, interesting muscle is found on the back of the ribs, in what is sometimes called the calotte where I am in Quebec. It's the extension of the belly/side on the loin, the part near the shoulder. Called *secretos* in Latin countries — it is a "secret" hidden cut and an excellent flat muscle to grill if you can find it.

Learn more: Sometimes, the shoulder is separated between the 3rd and 4th rib to get more ribs on the loin/the rib end (they are still considered loin ribs). The cut can also be made between the 5th and 6th ribs; it will then contain fewer ribs.

WHOLESALE CUT: LOIN	
Retail cut	**Cooking method**
Bone-in center-cut chops (with tenderloin)	Grill, sauté
Sirloin chops	Grill, sauté
Center-cut chops	Grill, sauté
Frenched center-cut chops	Grill, sauté
Butterflied chops	Grill, sauté
Back ribs	Braise, grill, simmer
Kabob cubes	Grill, sauté
Tenderloin	Braise, fry, grill, roast, sauté
Rib roast (bone-in or boneless) - *Individual muscle: secretos*	Braise, roast *Braise, grill, simmer, sauté*
Frenched rib roast (rack of pork)	Braise, roast
Crown roast	Braise, roast
Bone-in center-cut loin roast	Braise, roast
Boneless center-cut loin roast	Braise, roast
Sirloin roast (with bone or boneless)	Braise, simmer, roast
Tenderloin medallions	Grill

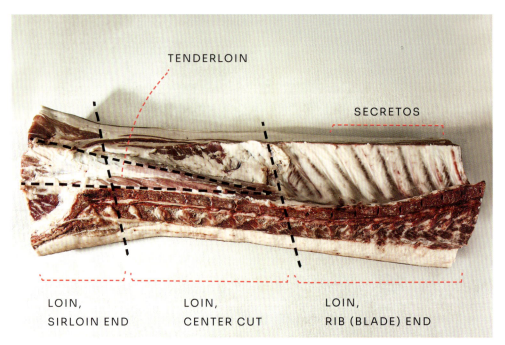

TENDERLOIN

SECRETOS

LOIN,
SIRLOIN END

LOIN,
CENTER CUT

LOIN,
RIB (BLADE) END

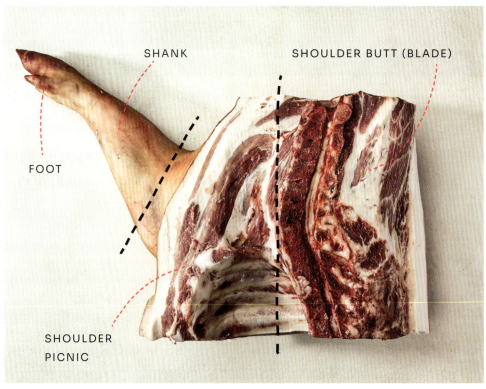

SHANK

SHOULDER BUTT (BLADE)

FOOT

SHOULDER
PICNIC

2 – SHOULDER

This wholesale cut can be separated in various ways; the most common contains two parts: The shoulder picnic is the part of the shoulder containing the humerus. It is cut from the end of the shank to the point where the humerus connects with the scapulum (see bottom photo, opposite). Once the shoulder picnic portion is removed, the butt (also called the Boston butt or blade) contains the rest of the shoulder. Here we find the scapulum, several ribs and some vertebrae. The shoulder blade bone and vertebrae can be removed, while retaining the scapulum for a bone-in butt (blade) roast. The capicola is a group of muscles in the butt (blade). Round in shape, it's the cut used to make the popular Italian cured meat by the same name. For pork, the foreshank is also found in the shoulder primal cut, but it is often removed by the butcher to be sold separately. Unlike beef, pork shanks (or hocks) can be purchased and cooked with the foot.

For connoisseurs: Those who love barbecue and pulled pork are very familiar with the "money muscle." It is found at the end of the whole shoulder blade. The presa, another small muscle in the blade, has an oval shape and is very red, so it's easily confused with beef. Perfect for grilling, the presa is tender and moist. The pluma is another small, hidden muscle, found in the shoulder butt (blade), adjoining the loin and it's delicious grilled. This cut gets its name from its resemblance to a feather.

More info: The shoulder can be separated between the 3rd and 4th rib or between the 5th and 6th rib. This gives a longer or shorter loin, as needed.

WHOLESALE CUT: SHOULDER	
Retail cut	**Cooking method**
Pork shoulder chop (rib section)	Braise, grill, simmer
Pork shoulder chop (without rib)	Braise, grill, simmer
Whole shoulder (without shank)	Braise, simmer
Foreshank with foot	Braise, simmer
Foreshank with skin, whole	Braise, simmer
Foreshank with rind, sliced	Braise, simmer
Osso buco-style shank (without rind and sliced)	Braise, simmer
Shoulder butt (blade), bone-in	Braise, simmer
Foot	Simmer
Shoulder picnic roast, bone-in or boneless	Braise, simmer
Shoulder blade capicola roast (boneless) - *Individual muscle: money muscle* - *Individual muscle: pluma* - *Individual muscle: presa*	Braise, fry, simmer, roast *Braise, grill, simmer, sauté* *Grill, simmer, sauté* *Grill, simmer, sauté*
Shoulder butt (blade) roast, bone-in or boneless	Braise, simmer, roast
Shoulder butt (blade) chop, bone-in	Braise, grill, simmer
Shoulder butt (blade) chop, boneless - *Group of muscles: capicola*	Braise, grill, simmer *Braise, grill, simmer, roast, sauté*

3 – BELLY/SIDE

This is exactly what it sounds like — the belly of the animal. It's from the belly/side that we get succulent bacon and salt pork. It is often used for porchetta and Asian pork belly, as its rind can become crispy when cooked. The belly/side contains the spareribs (side ribs). When these are removed and trimmed into a rectangular shape and the cartilage removed, they become St. Louis style ribs. They are very popular in the world of barbecue.

For connoisseurs: Pork bavette (sirloin flap meat), which is smaller than the beef version, is also found here. It is not well known, but it is delicious grilled on the barbecue. The flank muscle corresponds to flank steak for beef and can also be grilled or stewed. It is, however, less tender than bavette.

WHOLESALE CUT: BELLY/SIDE	
Retail cut	**Cooking method**
Spareribs (side ribs)	Braise, grill, simmer, roast
Whole flank sub-primal -*Individual muscle: bavette* -*Individual muscle: flank*	Braise, simmer, roast *Grill, simmer, sauté* *Grill, simmer, sauté*
Bone-in belly (whole)	Braise, grill, simmer, roast
Bone-in belly, (sliced)	Braise, grill, simmer
Pork belly slices, boneless (with or without rind)	Grill, sauté

4 – THE LEG

Popular in the world of charcuterie, the leg is often turned into ham, sausages and prosciutto. Besides these tasty cured meats, the leg offers a wide range of excellent cuts. As in cattle, here we find the round/hip, the rump, the sirloin and the sirloin tip. The parts of the leg are often turned into roasts and slices for grilling. Butchers offer cuts such as scaloppini/cutlets, strips, medallions, paupiettes (stuffed bundles) and grilling or stewing cubes. A slice of whole leg is sometimes called rouelle, because of its wheel shape. The hindshank is included in the leg primal cut. The shank, also called the hock, can be kept whole or cut into pieces; with the rind, it is often used for pig's feet stew, a traditional Quebec dish. More and more, we see it with the rind removed and sliced. It is then called osso buco-style shank.

For connoisseurs: The spider muscle, sometimes considered offal, is found in the leg; it runs along the inside of the aitch bone. This very small pork cut is a choice piece that is rather hard to find.

WHOLESALE CUT: LEG	
Retail cut	**Cooking method**
Grilling cubes	Grill, sauté
Stewing cubes	Braise, simmer
Scaloppini/cutlets	Grill, sauté
Whole leg (boneless or not)	Braise, simmer, roast
Hindshank (hock, with foot)	Braise, simmer
HIndshank (without foot)	Braise, simmer
Strips	Grill, sauté
Medallions	Grill
Eye of round roast	Grill, roast
Osso buco style shank (without rind, sliced)	Braise, simmer
Paupiettes (stuffed bundles)	Grill, simmer, roast
Fresh ham (leg roast), sirloin half	Braise, simmer, roast
Fresh ham (leg roast) shank end	Braise, simmer, roast
Inside fresh ham (leg) roast (boneless)	Braise, simmer, roast
Outside fresh ham (leg) roast (boneless)	Braise, simmer, roast
Sirloin tip fresh ham (leg) roast *- Individual muscle: cap (stewing cubes)* *- Individual muscle: eye/side (scaloppini/cutlets)* *- Individual muscle: round/center (roast, medallions, slices)*	Braise, simmer, roast *Braise, simmer* *Grill, sauté* *Grill, simmer, roast, sauté*
Fresh ham (leg slices), mechanically tenderized or not	Grill
Whole leg steak *- Individual muscle: spider*	Braise, grill, simmer, roast *Sauté, grill*
Outside fresh ham (leg) steaks	Grill, simmer
Inside fresh ham (leg) steaks *- Individual muscle: inside round cap (stewing cubes)* *- Individual muscle: adductor* *- Individual muscle: bullet*	Grill, simmer *Braise, simmer* *Grill, roast, sauté* *Grill, roast, sauté*
Sirloin tip fresh ham (leg) steaks	Grill
Sirloin fresh ham (leg) steaks	Grill

5 – HEAD AND TAIL

A pig's head, unlike veal or beef, can be bought whole. Fun fact about pork: the entire animal can be eaten, from the snout to the tail! The head contains several small muscles, such as the cheeks, which are delicious and full of collagen. When stewed, they become tender and juicy (though don't confuse them with jowls: see For connoisseurs, below). The tongue, even though it is a muscle, is often considered red offal. The whole head can be boiled to make head cheese. The snout and meat from the head are also often turned into *museau torchon*, a gelatinous charcuterie that is very popular in France, but is not well-known in North America. Pig ears are also cooked. They can be fried, used to make soup and even sautéed.

For connoisseurs: Pork jowl is the equivalent of a double chin. The jowl is fatty and can be compared to pork belly. Italians dry it and use it to make charcuterie called guanciale, and it's also used in traditional recipes like carbonara.

Although it doesn't contain much meat, pork tail is rich in collagen, and like the feet, it is used to make stock, soups, fricassees and stews. Before cooking the tail, it is very important to brush it well and rinse it in water. In Asian cuisine, the tail is highly prized for its high collagen content and very low price.

WHOLESALE CUT: HEAD AND TAIL	
Retail cut	**Cooking method**
Jowl	Braise, simmer
Cheek	Simmer
Tongue	Braise, grill, simmer
Ears	Simmer
Tail (in pieces or whole)	Simmer
Whole head	Braise, grill, simmer

The meat cuts in this book are based on French-Canadian artisan butchery cuts, sometimes enriched with European French artisan butchery cuts, and they don't always match up exactly to US or Canadian English-language meat cuts and standard terminology. The appendix at the back of the book will help guide you, providing translations and possible alternate names for cuts, and you can visit your local butcher who may be able to help answer your questions.

PORK RILLETTES +
DATES

Where pork butt (blade) comes from: shoulder

PORK RILLETTES + DATES

Where pork butt (blade) comes from: shoulder

88

CARNIVORE

I like freezing these economical rillettes so I always have some on hand.

Makes
6 cups (1.5 L)
Prep time – 45 min
Cooking time – 5 hours 30 min
Refrigeration – 24 hours

Rillettes

¾ cup (180 mL) lard

1 whole pork shank, fore or hind, (with rind and bone), in large pieces

4½ lbs (2 kg) boneless pork shoulder butt (blade), whole or in large pieces

3 large onions, diced

1 cup (250 mL) white wine

2 bay leaves

1 sprig of thyme

1 garlic clove, shoot removed, crushed

3 whole cloves

Salt and pepper

Date purée

2½ cups (625 mL) pitted dried dates, coarsely chopped

1 cup (250 mL) water

2 tbsp (30 mL) lemon juice

1. Preheat the oven to 250ºF (125ºC).

2. **Rillettes.** In a Dutch oven or other oven-proof heavy pan, over medium-high heat, melt lard. When it is hot, sauté the shank, shoulder and onions for about 5 minutes.

3. Add white wine, bay leaves, thyme, garlic and cloves. Generously season with salt and pepper to your taste.

4. Cover and bake for about 5 hours, or until the meat is tender and shreds easily (if it doesn't, simply continue cooking until it does). Stir every hour so the mixture doesn't stick to the bottom of the pan.

5. Remove the meat and let cool on a baking sheet. Strain the cooking juices through a sieve and set aside. Let the fat float to the top.

6. **Date purée.** In a saucepan, over high heat, boil all the ingredients for 5 to 10 minutes, or until stewed. Set aside.

7. In a large bowl, shred the cooled meat. Add cooking fat gradually (skimmed from the top of the cooking liquid), stirring until the texture is dense and very juicy.

8. Transfer the meat mixture to ramekins or a pâté mold, filling them a little less than half full. Press down with a fork. Add an even layer of date purée, about 1 inch (2.5 cm) thick, then top with another layer of the meat mixture.

9. Cover with plastic wrap and refrigerate 24 hours before diving in! Store in the fridge for up to 1 week or freeze for several months.

CAPICOLA MEDALLIONS +
PINEAPPLE

Serves
4 sensible eaters or
2 foolish eaters
Prep time – 25 min
Cooking time – 30 min
Resting time – 5 to 10 min

Pineapple barbecue sauce

¾ cup (175 mL) pineapple juice
¾ cup (175 mL) packed brown sugar
¾ cup (175 mL) ketchup
1 garlic clove, shoot removed, minced
2 tbsp (30 mL) Worcestershire sauce
½ tsp (2 mL) onion salt
Hot pepper sauce

Medallions

4 slices of pineapple, core removed
4 slices pork shoulder blade capicola
  roast (or boneless blade/butt roast),
  2 inches (5 cm) thick
4 maraschino cherries
8 slices bacon (optional)
Salt to taste

Materials

Butcher's twine
Brush

1. Pineapple barbecue sauce. In a saucepan, over medium-high heat, bring all the ingredients to a boil. Reduce the heat to low and simmer for 10 minutes, stirring often, or until the mixture forms a sauce texture. Set aside.

2. Medallions. Place one slice of pineapple on each slice of pork and place a cherry in the center. If desired, wrap 2 slices of bacon around the outside of each medallion (like a filet mignon). Tie together with twine, making a bow on top (like a present!).

3. Preheat a barbecue to high on just one side of the grill; for a charcoal grill, use a charcoal chimney starter to get glowing coals and place it at one end of the grill.

4. Evenly salt the meat. Sear the meat on the grill over direct heat or place directly in the coals. Cook until browned on all sides, turning halfway through cooking. If pieces of charcoal stick to the meat, remove them with tongs.

5. Continue cooking over indirect heat (if over charcoal, put the barbecue grill back in). With a brush, baste the meat with pineapple barbecue sauce every 3 minutes. Cook for 15 minutes, or until the internal temperature reaches 145°F (63°C) for medium-rare or to desired doneness (see page 18).

6. Let rest 5 to 10 minutes before serving.

Note

This recipe is just as tasty baked in the oven. Preheat oven to 275°F (135°C). Sear the medallions over high heat in an oiled oven-proof skillet. Once they are browned on all sides, baste with pineapple barbecue sauce and bake in the oven for about 30 minutes or until the internal temperature reaches 145°F (63°C) for medium-rare or to desired doneness (see page 18).

PAUPIETTES + MUSHROOMS + CREAM

Where the inside round comes from: the leg

Serves – 6 relaxed people or 4 resolute people
Prep time – 1 hour   **Cooking time** – 55 min   **Resting time** – 5 min

Pork stuffing

2 tbsp (30 mL) cold water

1 tsp (5 mL) salt

¼ tsp (1 mL) pepper

¼ tsp (1 mL) ground nutmeg

¼ tsp (1 mL) ground ginger

1 lb (450 g) ground pork (see Notes, page 94)

Six 2-inch (5 cm) cubes of aged Cheddar cheese

Paupiettes

6 large pork inside leg scaloppini, about 4 oz (125 g)
  each (or scaloppini cut from tenderloin or boneless loin)

Caul fat (see Notes, page 94)

6 slices of bacon

Salt

Mushrooms and cream sauce

2 tbsp (30 mL) vegetable oil

3 cups (750 mL) sliced mushrooms

2 tbsp (30 mL) butter

2 garlic cloves, shoots removed, finely chopped

1 shallot, finely chopped

1 cup (250 mL) white wine

Salt and pepper

1 cup (250 mL) heavy or whipping (35%) cream

Chopped parsley (optional)

Materials

Butcher's twine

Instructions: see next page

1. Preheat the oven to 350°F (180°C).

2. **Pork stuffing.** In a bowl, mix the water with salt, pepper, nutmeg and ginger, then add the ground pork. With your hands, mix thoroughly to spread the spices throughout the meat. Divide the stuffing into six equal portions and form each one into a ball.

3. Insert a cheese cube in the center of each ball. Close up the ball and roll it so the cheese won't escape during cooking.

4. **Paupiettes.** Wrap each stuffed ball in a scaloppini and cover with caul fat. Wrap each paupiette in a slice of bacon. Tie the twine around the bacon, pulling tight so everything stays in place and the paupiette is nice and round.

5. Evenly salt the paupiettes to your taste. Place on a rimmed baking sheet. Bake for 40 minutes, or until the internal temperature reaches 160°F (71°C). No need to add any liquid: the bacon and caul fat will take care of that! Let rest for 5 minutes.

6. **Mushrooms and cream sauce.** In a skillet, over high heat, heat oil and sauté mushrooms until they begin to brown. Add butter, garlic and shallot. Continue cooking for 2 to 3 minutes. Deglaze with white wine, scraping the bottom with a wooden spoon to get all the browned bits. Season with salt and pepper to taste. Boil until the liquid is reduced by half. Add cream, stir and let thicken for about 5 minutes.

7. To serve, make a bed of mushrooms and cream sauce on individual plates and place the paupiette on top. Garnish with parsley, if desired.

Notes

You will get better results with pork that has been ground just once. At the grocery store, ground pork has been ground twice or even three times. It is therefore best to visit your butcher.

Caul fat is a membrane found in the abdomen and it's very useful for wrapping mixtures, especially in charcuterie. Fairly fatty, it melts during cooking, basting the meat. You will find it frozen in ball form at butcher shops. Ask your meat pro how much you need for this recipe.

FRENCHED PORK RIB CHOPS + BUTTERNUT SQUASH + LARDONS

Where pork chops come from: the loin

Serves – 4 moderate eaters or 2 extravagant eaters
Prep time – 1 hour   **Tempering** – 15 min   **Cooking time** – 2 hours   **Resting time** – 10 min

Puréed and sautéed squash

1 large butternut squash
1 tbsp (15 mL) vegetable oil
Salt and pepper
¼ cup (60 mL) butter
8 oz (225 g) lardons, cut into matchsticks
1 onion, chopped
A few sage leaves

Toasted squash seeds

2 tbsp (30 mL) pure maple syrup
1 tbsp (15 mL) vegetable oil
2 mL (½ tsp) French 4-spice mix (*quatre épices*)
Salt

Pork chops

4 Frenched pork loin rib chops, each 7 oz (200 g)
3 tbsp (45 mL) vegetable oil

Instructions: see next page

1. Preheat the oven to 300°F (150°C).

2. **Puréed and sautéed squash.** Cut squash in half lengthwise. Scrape out seeds, rinse and reserve seeds. Set one squash half aside. Make slits in the flesh side of the other squash half. Place on a large sheet of foil. Coat with oil, then sprinkle with salt and pepper to your taste. Wrap foil around the squash to enclose and bake for about 1 hour, or until the squash is tender.

3. Meanwhile, peel the reserved squash half. Dice. Set aside.

4. With a spoon, remove the hot flesh of the cooked squash from the skin; discard the skin. Using a food processor or blender, purée with the butter. Season with salt and pepper to your taste. Set aside; keep warm.

5. In a skillet, over medium-high heat, sauté lardons and onion until golden brown. Add diced squash and sage leaves. Sauté until squash is tender and nicely browned. Set aside.

6. **Toasted squash seeds.** In a medium bowl, combine maple syrup, oil, spice mix and salt to your taste. Add reserved squash seeds and mix well. In a skillet, over medium-high heat, sauté seasoned squash seeds until golden and crispy. Set aside; keep warm.

7. **Pork chops.** Let the pork chops sit at room temperature on a wire rack for 15 minutes.

8. Preheat the oven to 300°F (150°C).

9. In an oven-safe skillet, over high heat, sear the pork chops in the oil. Bake for 10 minutes, or until the internal temperature reaches 142°F (61°C). Let rest for 10 minutes.

10. To serve, place the squash purée in the middle of a platter. Arrange the pork chops on top, then the sautéed squash. Garnish with toasted squash seeds.

PORK TENDERLOIN +
DRYING + SIMPLE

Where pork tenderloin comes from: the loin

My bestie for cocktails on the balcony in summertime. I love to eat it with melon, much like we do with prosciutto. I add mozzarella and fresh mint: de-li-cious!

Serves
5 reasonable people or
3 off-the-wall people
Prep time – 20 min
Refrigeration – 12 hours
Drying – about 21 days

1 large pork tenderloin, about 1 lb (450 g)

Coarse salt, enough to thoroughly cover the pork tenderloin

Your choice of seasonings: ground pepper, steak spices, curry powder, dried herbs (optional)

Equipment

Cheesecloth or paper towel

1. Trim the pork tenderloin well: remove the top nerve, white membrane (silver skin, see Notes) and all surface fat.

2. Place the tenderloin on a large glass plate and cover completely with coarse salt. Cover with plastic wrap and refrigerate for 12 hours or overnight.

3. Rinse the tenderloin in cold water and discard the salt. Dry the meat well with a tea towel or paper towel.

4. If desired, coat the tenderloin well with your choice of seasonings.

5. Wrap the tenderloin in cheesecloth. Place on a large plate and set on the bottom shelf in the fridge.

6. Let dry for 2 to 3 weeks. During the drying time, turn the pork tenderloin every 3 or 4 days.

7. Once the meat is very dry (see Notes), cut across the grain into very thin slices and enjoy.

Notes

Silver skin is a type of connective tissue that covers the muscle. This membrane is not fat: during cooking (or drying), it doesn't melt, it hardens. That's why we remove it.

The pork tenderloin is ready when it is dry right to the center. If, after slicing it, you notice that this isn't the case, don't panic! Simply re-wrap in cheesecloth and put it back in the fridge; let it continue drying for a few extra days. Warning: if you notice any kind of mold or the tenderloin is sticky, do not eat the meat.

SPARERIBS + BABY-CUE SAUCE + APRICOTS

Where ribs come from: flank

Serves – 3 calm people or 2 less calm people or 1 not-at-all calm person
Prep time – 1 hour **Tempering** – 15 min **Cooking time** – about 5 hours

Ribs

1 whole rack St. Louis-style pork spareribs (side ribs, center cut)
1⅔ cups (400 mL) unsweetened apple juice, divided
¼ cup (60 mL) butter, cut in 4 thin slices

Baby-cue sauce

2 jars (each 4 oz/128 mL) apricot baby food
½ cup (125 mL) chili sauce
⅓ cup (80 mL) white vinegar
½ cup (125 mL) packed brown sugar
2 garlic cloves, shoots removed, finely chopped
2 tbsp (30 mL) soy sauce
Hot pepper sauce to taste (optional)
Salt and pepper

Rub

¼ cup (60 mL) packed brown sugar
¼ cup (60 mL) smoked paprika
1 tbsp (15 mL) ground black pepper
2 tbsp (30 mL) onion salt
2 tbsp (30 mL) garlic salt
2 tsp (10 mL) celery salt

Equipment

Smoking wood chips
1 spray bottle
Foil
1 basting brush

1. Ribs. If necessary, square off the ribs by cutting the sternebrae to get an even rectangular piece. Remove the white membrane from the back of the ribs (silver skin: see Notes, page 98). Let sit at room temperature on a wire rack for 15 minutes.

2. Preheat the smoker or barbecue to 275°F (135°C) and set up to cook over indirect heat. Once the internal temperature of the smoker or barbecue has been reached, add your choice of smoking wood.

3. Baby-cue sauce. In a saucepan, over medium-high heat, cook all the ingredients for 10 minutes, stirring often, or until brown sugar is dissolved and the sauce is smooth. Remove from the heat and set aside.

4. Rub. In a bowl, combine all the ingredients well.

5. Season the ribs with ⅓ cup (80 mL) of the rub and place them on the grill.

6. Fill the spray bottle with apple juice, reserving 2 tbsp (30 mL).

7. Smoke the ribs over indirect heat for about 2 hours or until nicely browned and smoked. Spray with apple juice as needed so the ribs don't dry out.

8. On a large sheet of foil, arrange the slices of butter in a line. Add 1 tbsp (15 mL) of the rub and the 2 tbsp (30 mL) reserved apple juice. Place the ribs meat side down on the butter (bone side up) and close up the foil to make a pouch. Cover with another layer of foil to seal as tightly as possible.

9. Return the meat to the smoker and continue cooking over indirect heat for about 2 hours or until you can see the meat pulling away from the ends of the bones (check by carefully opening the pouch) and the internal temperature of meat reaches 205°F (96°C).

10. Unwrap the ribs, put them back on the grill, then increase the temperature of the smoker to 300°F (150°C). With a brush, baste with baby-cue sauce to taste and smoke for about 1 hour.

> **Note**
> Keep the leftover rub for chicken dishes, potatoes, etc.

PORK CHEEKS CONFIT + TARRAGON DIJONNAISE

Where the cheek comes from: the head

Pork cheek confit is packed with flavor. Like duck leg confit, it is a perfect addition to your salads, charcuterie platters, sandwiches, stews, quick sautés and much more! Try them with this tarragon Dijonnaise: a delight!

Serves
6 shy people or
4 outgoing people
Prep time – 5 min
Cooking time – 2 hours

Pork cheeks

2¼ lbs (1 kg) lard

18 pork cheeks (see Notes)

3 sprigs of rosemary

1 bay leaf

4 garlic cloves, shoots removed, crushed

1 tsp (5 mL) coarse salt

1 tsp (5 mL) pepper

Tarragon Dijonnaise

⅔ cup (150 mL) mayonnaise

1½ tbsp (22 mL) whole-grain mustard

1 tbsp (15 mL) Dijon mustard

1 tsp (5 mL) honey or maple syrup

1 garlic clove, shoot removed, chopped (optional)

Fresh tarragon, finely chopped, to taste

Salt and pepper

1. **Pork cheeks.** In a saucepan, over medium-high heat, melt lard. Add pork cheeks, rosemary, bay leaf, garlic, salt and pepper. Simmer over low heat for about 2 hours. Do not bring to a boil. The cheeks are ready when they are tender and can be shredded with a fork.

2. Gently remove the cheeks from the cooking fat and place them in a sieve set over a bowl to drain. Set the meat aside on a plate.

3. With the sieve, strain the cooking fat into a sealable container to use in other recipes or to store the pork cheeks confit in the fridge (see Notes).

4. **Tarragon Dijonnaise.** In a bowl, combine all the ingredients and stir well until smooth.

5. To serve, place a few dabs of Dijonnaise on a plate and place the cheeks on top.

Notes

You can keep the thin membrane on the pork cheek; it's easy to remove by pulling it after cooking. You don't even have to remove it before eating: it's tasty!

Pork cheek confit can keep for up to a month in the fridge when covered with the strained cooking fat.

Lamb

Lamb is a one-of-a-kind meat and is perfect for special occasions! Its flavor is unique and distinctive — totally unlike other meats. As with all farm animals, what the animal eats will determine its flavor on the plate. So, a grass-fed lamb will not have the same flavor, color or texture as a grain-fed lamb.

Like veal, lamb is "young" meat: a baby sheep. Given its small size, there are fewer cuts and fewer individual muscles. To give you a sense of this, lamb bavette (sirloin flap meat) is like something from *Alice in Wonderland*: it is so tiny, it's barely one bite.

Lamb, which is more expensive than some other meats, contains exceptional cuts such as the leg, the rack and the loin chops. Even the less prestigious cuts are delicious! Don't underestimate the shanks, the shoulder and the neck.

Where I live in Quebec, there are three types of farm lambs, classified according to their weight: suckling (milk-fed) lamb (under 65 lbs/30 kg), light lamb (between 65 and 79 lbs/30 and 35 kg) and heavy lamb, also called Quebec lamb (up to 130 lbs/60 kg/). There are many lamb breeds, such as Hampshire, Berrichon, Quercy, Avranchin and Cotentin (raised in salt marshes). This might be different in the US or in other parts of Canada.

Lamb is a SHEAR delight with a EWE-nique flavor!

LAMB

CUTS

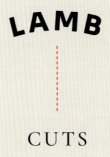

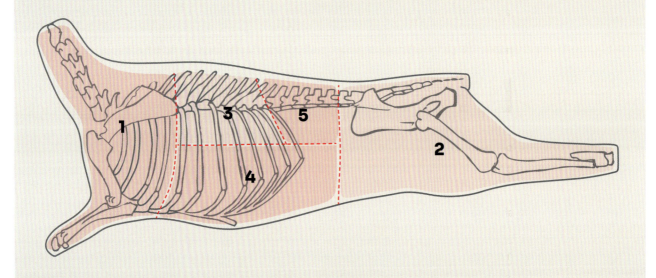

1 – FRONT
2 – LEG
3 – RIB (RACK)
4 – FLANK
5 – LOIN

1 – FRONT

Here we find several cuts: the neck, the shoulder rib chops (the first five ribs before the rack)*, breast, shoulder and foreshank. The neck is tasty and used mostly sliced with the bone in to make stews, tajines and soups because it needs longer cooking. The neck can also be completely deboned to make stewing cubes or left whole for grilling. By the way, it's only with lamb that it's tender enough to grill the neck. Lamb shoulder is sometimes sold as a whole piece and includes the first five ribs and several vertebrae. In that case it is called lamb blade (also called square cut lamb shoulder), and it's usually sliced. The shoulder can also be separated from the ribs and vertebrae leaving only the scapulum and the scapulo-humeral joint. It can be purchased whole with the bone in, boneless, as a roast, sliced with the bone in, and as boneless cubes. Attached to the shoulder, the foreshank has less meat than the hindshank because it is a muscle that works much harder. It is often sold whole, but it can also be boneless or sliced, like with osso buco. When the shoulder is removed with the shank, without the ribs and vertebrae, it's called the shoulder with shank. The front of the lamb, as with pork, can vary: it can be cut between the 3rd and 5th ribs to get a rack containing more or fewer ribs (according to preference.)

*Note: the French call these *côtes découvertes*, meaning "discovered" or "found" chops.

WHOLESALE CUT: FRONT	
Retail cut	**Cooking method**
Whole neck, bone in	Braise, simmer
Whole neck, boneless	Braise, grill, simmer
Sliced neck	Braise, grill, simmer
Bone-in lamb shoulder roast	Braise, simmer
Foreshank	Braise, simmer
Flank/breast, in pieces	Braise, grill, simmer
Shoulder with shank	Braise, simmer
Boneless lamb shoulder roast	Braise, simmer, roast
Shoulder blade (whole) - *Individual muscle: flat iron*	Braise, simmer *Braise, grill, simmer, sauté*
Shoulder arm chops	Grill, simmer
Shoulder blade chops	Braise, grill, simmer
Shoulder rib chops	Braise, grill, simmer, sauté

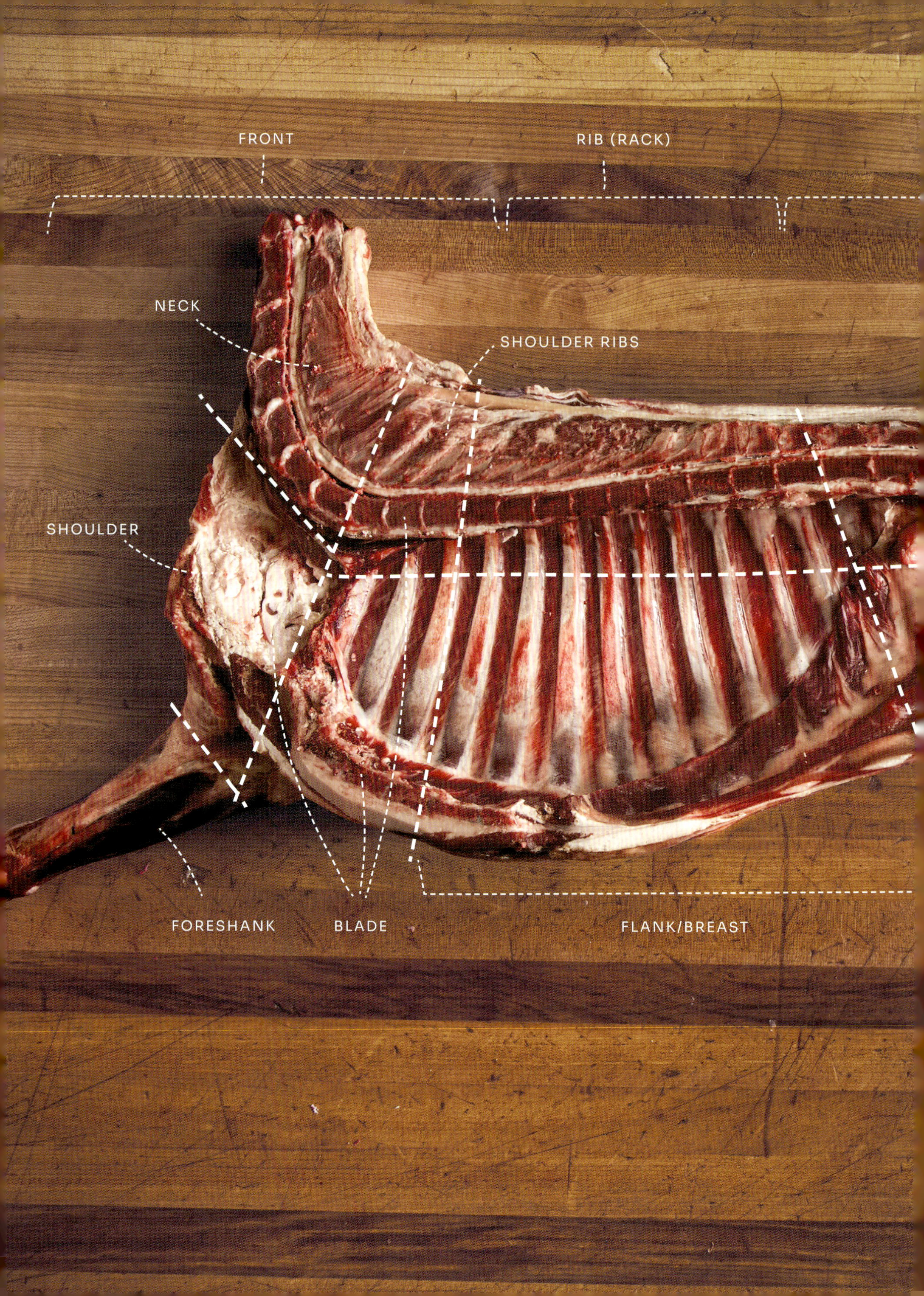

FRONT

RIB (RACK)

NECK

SHOULDER RIBS

SHOULDER

FORESHANK

BLADE

FLANK/BREAST

LOIN/LOIN CHOPS

LEG

HINDSHANK

2 – THE LEG

This festive cut is traditionally cooked at Easter or Christmas. The leg is the equivalent of the animal's thigh. When whole, this cut includes an extension of the sirloin end, which begins right after the last chop of the loin and ends at the tip of the hip bone. If the sirloin end is removed, you'll have a short cut leg that can be sliced for grilling. Leg, either whole or short cut, can be cut as a boneless roast, whole with the bone in, and sometimes semi-boneless. The leg can be processed, muscle by muscle, to make pieces for grilling or kabob cubes.

For connoisseurs: The hindshank has more meat than the foreshank. In French, a lamb hindshank is called *souris d'agneau* (mouse lamb), because its shape calls to mind that of a mouse.

WHOLESALE CUT: LEG	
Retail cut	**Cooking method**
Tenderloin (head only)	Grill, sauté
Whole leg (bone in or boneless)	Braise, simmer, roast
Frenched long leg	Braise, simmer, roast
Boneless leg roast	Braise, simmer, roast
Shank-end leg roast	Braise, simmer, roast
Shank-end leg roast with hindshank	Braise, simmer, roast
Butt-portion leg roast	Braise, simmer, roast
Sirloin roast	Braise, simmer, roast
Hindshank	Braise, simmer, roast
Boneless hindshank	Braise, simmer
Center cut leg steak (centre slice leg steak)	Braise, grill, roast, sauté
Sliced hindshank, osso buco–style	Braise, simmer, roast
Sirloin chop	Braise, grill, roast, sauté

The meat cuts in this book are based on French-Canadian artisan butchery cuts, sometimes enriched with European French artisan butchery cuts, and they don't always match up exactly to US or Canadian English-language meat cuts and standard terminology. The appendix at the back of the book will help guide you, providing translations and possible alternate names for cuts, and you can visit your local butcher who may be able to help answer your questions.

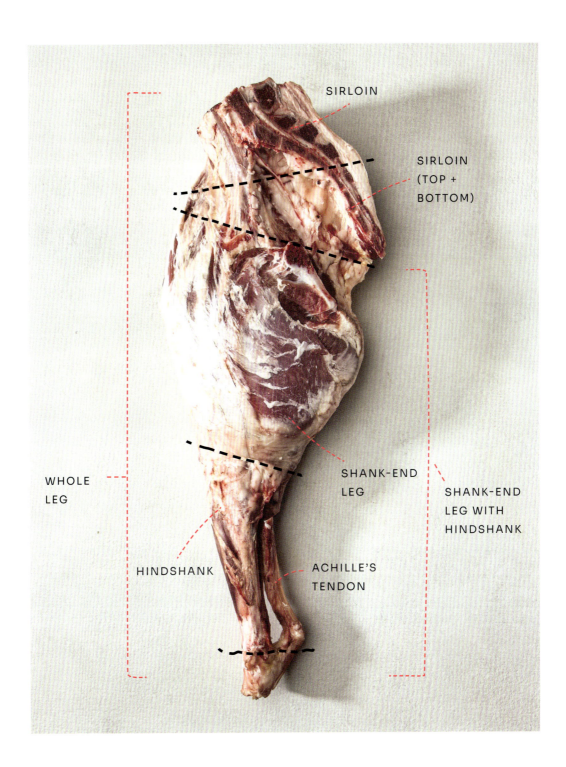

SIRLOIN

SIRLOIN
(TOP +
BOTTOM)

WHOLE
LEG

SHANK-END
LEG

SHANK-END
LEG WITH
HINDSHANK

HINDSHANK

ACHILLE'S
TENDON

3 – THE RIB (RACK)

This is one of the most popular lamb cuts. It is most often sold with the meat cleaned off the ribs, which is called a Frenched lamb rib roast or a Frenched rack of lamb, or cut between ribs into chops. It can also be sold without the bones being cleaned and with the rib portion of the flank attached, a version that is, ironically, more popular in France. The butcher can prepare a crown roast with the whole rib (or rack) with the bones cleaned, a very elegant way to enjoy this cut.

For connoisseurs: The rib (or rack) contains three different cuts of rib chops: shoulder-end (fattier), tenderloin chops and center cut chops.

WHOLESALE CUT: RIB (RACK)	
Retail cut	**Cooking method**
Rib roast (rack of lamb)	Grill, roast
Rib chops	Grill, sauté
Frenched rib chops	Grill, sauté
Crown roast	Braise, roast
Boneless ribeye	Grill, sauté

4 – THE FLANK

It is often sold deboned and you might see it called lamb belly. Several boneless flanks can be rolled and tied together; it can then be cooked as a roast or sliced. Boneless rolled flank roast is delicious grilled or smoked and it can also be simmered or used in stews. Sometimes, the bones and vertebrae are left in; then the flank is grilled whole.

WHOLESALE CUT: FLANK	
Retail cut	**Cooking method**
Spareribs (flank sideribs)	Braise, grill, simmer
Whole bone-in flank - *Individual muscle: sirloin flap meat (very small)* - *Individual muscle: flank steak (very small)*	Braise, grill, roast *Grill, sauté* *Grill, sauté*
Boneless rolled flank roast	Braise, roast
Stuffed boneless rolled flank roast	Braise, roast
Sliced flank, bone in or boneless	Braise, grill (boneless), roast, sauté (boneless)
Sliced flank, rolled and stuffed	Braise, grill, roast, sauté

5 – THE LOIN

This cut includes part of the tenderloin (the head portion is found in the sirloin) and the loin. When cut into chops, it's the equivalent of a T-bone but much smaller and they are called lamb loin chops. These chops are usually sliced to the thickness of one vertebra, and they are perfect for grilling on the barbecue in summer, like other cuts from the loin.

For connoisseurs: The two sides of the animal's loin are sometimes kept intact at the spinal column, which is called *baron d'agneau* in French, or saddle (though it's called by many different names worldwide). You can find the saddle as double loin chops or as a tied boneless roast.

WHOLESALE CUT: LOIN	
Retail cut	**Cooking method**
Lamb loin chop with flank (see Note, page 123)	Grill, sauté
Lamb loin chop (without tenderloin)	Grill, sauté
Double loin chop (saddle)	Grill, sauté
Loin chop	Grill, sauté
Lamb tenderloin (without head)	Grill, sauté
Flank (partial)	Braise, grill, simmer, roast, sauté
Bone-in loin roast	Grill
Boneless loin roast	Grill, roast, sauté
Double boneless loin roast (saddle)	Braise, roast

LAMB SHOULDER CONFIT + PRUNES + GARLIC + ROSEMARY

CARNIVORE

This very simple recipe showcases lamb shoulder. Plus, no need to wash the pan, as it cooks in a pouch (hurray!). Bonus: your whole house will smell good.

Serves
6 conventional people or
4 rebellious people
Prep time – 20 min
Cooking time – 5 hours

Vegetable oil to taste

1 bone-in lamb shoulder roast, about
  2¼ lbs (1 kg), fat trimmed

2 tsp (10 mL) salt

Pepper

12 garlic cloves, shoots removed, halved
  and divided

12 to 15 prunes, halved and divided

5 sprigs of rosemary, divided

1. Preheat the oven to 250°F (125°C).

2. Rub the lamb all over with oil, then sprinkle with the salt and pepper to your taste.

3. Place a large sheet of parchment paper or foil on a baking sheet; place half the garlic, half the prunes and 3 sprigs of rosemary on the paper. Place the lamb on top. Add the remaining garlic, prunes and rosemary on top of the meat.

4. Close up the parchment paper or foil to make a pouch. Cover with a layer of foil to seal it as tightly as possible.

5. Slide the foil pouch off the baking sheet into in the oven and bake for about 5 hours, until the meat is tender and can be shredded with a fork. Slide the pouch back onto the baking sheet to remove from the oven.

Note
You can open the pouch and keep cooking under the broiler until it browns to the color you want.

LEG OF LAMB + HAITIAN MARINADE + PIKLIZ COLESLAW

Where leg of lamb comes from: the leg

This is a recipe I love serving with bannann peze (fried green plaintains), an incredible side dish in Haitian cooking (see Note)! Keep the leftover marinade to season pork, chicken or vegetables, or even to brush your teeth . . . Ha-ha!

Serves
6 hungry kids or 4 hungry adults
Prep time – 20 min
Refrigeration – 2 to 24 hours
Tempering – 45 min
Cooking time – 1 hour 20 min
Resting time – 20 min

Haitian-style marinade

10 green onions, cut in chunks
1 onion, quartered
1 red bell pepper, quartered
3 garlic cloves, shoots removed
1 bunch of fresh parsley
⅓ cup (80 mL) vegetable oil
¼ cup (60 mL) white vinegar
2 seasoning cubes, such as Maggi
Scotch bonnet peppers (up to 4 for the real thing!)

Pikliz coleslaw

2 cups (500 mL) grated cabbage
1 cup (250 mL) grated carrots
1 red bell pepper, sliced finely
1 onion, sliced finely
1 green onion, chopped finely
Scotch bonnet pepper, chopped finely
¼ cup (60 mL) white vinegar
1 cup (250 mL) mayonnaise
Salt

Leg of lamb

1 short-cut semi-boneless leg of lamb, about 3 ½ lb (1.6 kg), tied

1. **Haitian-style marinade.** Using a food processor or blender, blend all the ingredients until smooth. Set aside.

2. **Pikliz coleslaw.** In a bowl, combine all the ingredients. Cover and refrigerate.

3. **Leg of lamb.** Unwrap the leg and pat it dry with a paper towel. Generously coat the lamb with marinade. Place the lamb in a large sealable container or on a deep platter and cover with plastic wrap. Let rest in the fridge for at least 2 hours or up to 24 hours.

4. Unwrap the lamb and let sit at room temperature on a wire rack for 45 minutes. (Reserve marinade.)

5. Preheat oven to 350°F (180°C).

6. Place the lamb with marinade in a large roasting pan and bake for about 1 hour and 20 minutes, or until the internal temperature reaches 135°F (57°C) for medium-rare or to the desired doneness (see page 18). Let rest for 20 minutes, covered with foil.

7. Slice the lamb and serve with the pikliz coleslaw.

Note

To make bannann peze, peel 3 green plantains and cut them diagonally in ½-inch (1 cm) chunks. Flatten the plantain pieces with a glass or rolling pin. Then fry them in oil until nicely browned. What a treat!

GRILLED LAMB LEG STEAK +
MINT CHIMICHURRI + RADISHES +
YELLOW BEETS

Where the steak comes from: the leg

Serves
2 discreet eaters or
1 in-your-face eater
Prep time – 25 min
Tempering – 30 min
Cooking time – 20 min
Resting time – 10 to 15 min

Steak

1 lamb center cut leg steak, about 1 lb
   (450 g) and 2½ inches (6 cm) thick
Salt

Mint chimichurri

1 cup (250 mL) fresh mint leaves
1 garlic clove, shoot removed
Zest of ½ lemon
Juice of 1 lemon
¼ cup (60 mL) extra virgin olive oil

Garnish

3 radishes, diced finely
1 small yellow beet, cooked and diced
   finely

1. Steak. Unwrap the lamb steak and let sit at room temperature on a wire rack for 30 minutes.
2. Mint chimichurri. In a food processor or blender, blend mint, garlic, lemon zest and juice until smooth. Drizzle in oil, blending to emulsify and get a smooth consistency. Set aside.
3. Preheat the barbecue to high on just one side of the grill; for a charcoal grill, use a charcoal chimney starter to get glowing coals and place it at one end of the grill.
4. Evenly salt the lamb to your taste. Place the lamb on the grill over direct heat or in the coals. Turn to sear all sides until nicely browned. Continue cooking over indirect heat, if needed, until the internal temperature reaches 131°F (55°C) for rare or to desired doneness (see page 18).
5. Let rest for 10 to 15 minutes.
6. Serve the sliced steak garnished with chimichurri, radishes and beets.

Note

This recipe also works on the stove. Preheat the oven to 325°F (160°C). Sear the lamb steak over high heat in 1 tbsp (15 mL) vegetable oil in an oven-proof skillet. Continue cooking in the oven for about 10 minutes, until the internal temperature reaches 131°F (55°C) for rare or to desired doneness (see page 18).

LAMB T-BONES + TABOULI + GARLIC YOGURT

Where the lamb loin chop comes from: the loin

This tabouli recipe was given to me by a taxi driver during a conversation about food during a ride through Montreal — I wrote it on the back of a receipt. I hung onto it because it's delicious. You can make tabouli a few hours or even a few days ahead: it will be even better! Thank you, Mr. Taxi Driver!

Serves
3 cautious people or
2 fearless people!
Prep time – 30 min
Cooking time – 20 min

Tabouli

2 medium onions, finely chopped

¾ tsp (3 mL) salt

¼ tsp (1 mL) black pepper

½ tsp (2 mL) ground sumac

Zest of ½ lemon

2 cups (500 mL) chopped fresh parsley

2 cups (500 mL) seeded and diced Italian tomatoes

¼ cup (60 mL) extra virgin olive oil

¼ cup (60 mL) fresh lemon juice

½ cup (125 mL) fine bulgur (or fine semolina)

Garlic yogurt

1 cup (250 mL) plain yogurt

2 small garlic cloves, shoots removed, chopped

½ tsp (2 mL) salt

T-bones

Salt

6 lamb loin chops (each 1 vertebra thick)

For serving (optional)

Pomegranate arils

Thin radish slices or cucumber ribbons

1. Tabouli. In a bowl, combine all the ingredients. Cover and refrigerate.

2. Garlic yogurt. In a bowl, combine all the ingredients. Cover and refrigerate.

3. Preheat the barbecue to high; for a charcoal grill, use a charcoal chimney starter to get glowing coals.

4. T-bones. Evenly salt the lamb chops to your taste. Grill for about 5 minutes on each side or until the internal temperature reaches 140°F (60°C) for medium-rare or to desired doneness (see page 18).

5. To serve, place a large spoonful of garlic yogurt in the middle of plate, arrange the lamb on top, then add the tabouli. Top with a few pomegranate arils, radish slices and/or cucumber ribbons, if desired.

Notes

Don't have a barbecue? You can also cook the lamb chops over high heat in an oiled skillet on the stovetop. Extra tabouli and garlic yogurt can be stored in the refrigerator for up to 2 days.

In France and Quebec, it is common to find lamb loin chops cut like a T-bone with a part of the flank attached and rolled as shown in the photo on page 122. Any bone-in lamb loin chops will work for this recipe.

RACK OF LAMB + BISCOFF COOKIES + FIGS + GOAT CHEESE

124

If you love a good crunch, you're in the right place! This recipe is so simple and so tasty!

CARNIVORE

Serves
3 little birds or 2 vultures
Prep time – 20 min
Tempering – 30 min
Cooking time – 20 to 25 min
Resting time – 10 min

Rack of lamb

1 lamb Frenched rib roast (Frenched rack of lamb), about 1½ lbs (700 g)
1 pkg (8.8 oz/250 g) Biscoff cookies
Salt
2 tbsp (30 mL) Dijon mustard

Greens, figs and goat cheese

2 cups (500 mL) arugula
2 tbsp (30 mL) extra virgin olive oil
Zest of ½ lemon
1 tsp (5 mL) lemon juice
Salt and pepper
⅓ cup (50 g) crumbled goat cheese
2 fresh figs, quartered
Pecan halves

1. Rack of lamb. Unwrap the lamb and let sit on a wire rack at room temperature for 30 minutes.
2. Preheat the oven to 425°F (220°C).
3. Coarsely crush the cookies (there should still be a few chunks). Set aside on a plate.
4. Evenly salt the lamb to your taste. With a brush, baste with Dijon mustard. Roll the lamb in the crumbs, pressing on the crumbs to make a crust over the entire surface.
5. Place in a roasting pan and bake for 20 to 25 minutes or until the crust is crispy and the internal temperature reaches 131°F (55°C) for medium-rare or to your desired doneness (page 18). Let rest 10 minutes.
6. Greens, figs and goat cheese. In a large bowl, combine arugula, olive oil, zest and lemon juice. Season with salt and pepper to your taste. Set aside.
7. Mash goat cheese until fairly smooth. Spread on the serving platter. Add the dressed greens and garnish with the quartered figs and pecans.
8. Place the lamb on top of the goat cheese.

LAMB FLANK + SMOKE

Where the flank comes from: the flank

Lamb flank (or belly) is not that popular, but I think it deserves to be cooked more often. Its meat-to-fat ratio is appealing. I like to thinly slice the leftovers to cook in a skillet, like bacon. It makes incredible lamb BLTs!

Serves
about 8 to 10 soldiers
Prep time – 25 min
Smoking – 3 to 4 hours
Resting time – 20 min

3 boneless lamb flanks (bellies), about 6⅔ lb (3 kg), trimmed
Salt
1 can (12 oz/355 mL) ginger ale

Equipment

Butcher's twine
Smoking wood chips
Spray bottle

1. On a clean worktop, line up the lamb flanks, skin side down, with the narrow sides end-to-end, overlapping by about 2 inches (5 cm), to make a long rectangle.

2. Generously and evenly salt the top side. Starting at one narrow end, roll up the meat tightly, jelly-roll style.

3. First tie together the two ends of the roll with solid shoelace knots (see Note) using the twine. Then tie the middle, the two sections between the middle and the end. Give the roast a uniform shape as you tie it.

4. Preheat the smoker or barbecue for cooking over indirect heat to 250°F (125°C). Once the internal temperature of the smoker or barbecue has been reached, add the smoking wood of your choice.

5. Fill the spray bottle with ginger ale.

6. Salt the outside of the roast well. Smoke over indirect heat for 3 to 4 hours, or until the internal temperature reaches 131°F (55°C) for rare or to your desired doneness (see page 18). Spray with ginger ale during smoking so the roast doesn't dry out. Let rest for 20 minutes.

7. Slice the roast and serve with a salad and potatoes, or in a pita with tzatziki sauce.

Note

A shoelace knot is simply the knot you make to tie your shoes. It's a frequently used term in butcher shops for those who don't know butcher's knots. It does the trick!

OFFAL

Offal is very popular in France. It is firmly rooted in French cuisine and is used in many local specialties. Although less popular in North America, I created a separate chapter for it because offal comes from a variety of animals and I also think it deserves to be explored in more depth when it comes to cooking.

Offal is divided into two categories: white offal, which requires blanching and whitening or cleaning before cooking, and red offal, which can be prepared as is. Some meaty muscles, such as the skirt, hanger and spider (or oyster), are often considered red offal. These muscles, also called "variety meats" or "organ meats," are located inside the chest cavity and are sometimes adjacent to offal. For example, hanger is found near the kidneys and kidney fat, which explains its strong flavor! Bone marrow can also be categorized as red offal.

Sweetbread, a "youth" gland, is found in young animals such as veal and lamb. It is divided into two categories: the elongated neck/throat sweetbread, and the heart sweetbreads, found nearer the heart, which is how it got its name. Given how rare it is, sweetbread is seen as fairly high end.

The animal's testicles are often called Rocky Mountain oysters and prairie oysters.

Finally, in poultry, the gizzard is a small digestive pouch used to grind up food or even small stones eaten by the bird! Gizzards are often made into preserves.

Despite the few extra steps needed to prepare offal, it is easy to cook, delicious and nutritious.

Here is a list of offal to try. Ask your butcher for guidance. It would be OFFAL to miss out on these tasty foods!

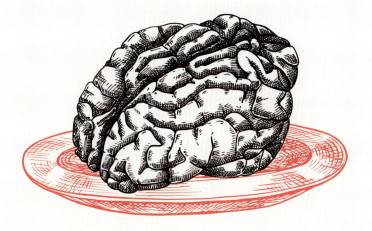

OFFAL	ANIMAL	CATEGORY
Bone marrow	Lamb	White
Brain	Lamb, rabbit, pork, veal	White
Caul fat or crépine	Pork	White
Cheek	Lamb, beef, pork, veal	Red
Foot	Lamb, pork, chicken, veal	White
Gizzard	Poultry	Red
Head	Lamb, rabbit, pork, veal	White
Intestine	Lamb, beef, pork	White
Kidney	Lamb, beef, rabbit, pork, veal	Red
Liver	Beef, rabbit, pork, veal, poultry	Red
Sweetbread	Lamb, veal	White
Tail	Pork, veal	Red
Tongue	Lamb, beef, pork, veal	Red
Testicles	Lamb	White
Tripe	Beef	White

CALF BRAIN POPCORN + MAYO + PESTO + PARMESAN

Delicious with an arugula salad!

Serves – 6 reasonable eaters or 4 aggressive eaters
Prep time – 1 hour   **Refrigeration** – 30 min   **Cooking time** – 20 min

Pesto Parmesan mayo

1 cup (250 mL) mayonnaise
¼ cup (60 mL) pesto
1 garlic clove, shoot removed, finely chopped
2 tbsp (30 mL) grated Parmesan
Salt and pepper

Calf brain popcorn

2 calf brains
Cold water
¼ cup (60 mL) white vinegar, divided
1 garlic clove, shoot removed, finely chopped
¼ cup (60 mL) butter
1 cup (250 mL) all-purpose flour
4 eggs
Salt and pepper
Cooking oil

1. **Pesto Parmesan mayo.** In a bowl, combine all the ingredients. Refrigerate.

2. **Calf brain popcorn.** In a large container, immerse the calf brains in cold water. Add 2 tbsp (30 mL) white vinegar. Place in the fridge for about 30 minutes.

3. Carefully rinse the brains in cold water and gently remove the membranes.

4. Fill a saucepan with water. Bring to a boil and add the remaining 2 tbsp (30 mL) white vinegar. Poach the brains for 5 minutes, then rinse in cold water. Sponge off excess liquid.

5. Cut the brains into bite-size pieces, place in a covered container and refrigerate.

6. In a saucepan, bring to a boil 1 cup (250 mL) water, the garlic and butter. Add flour and mix well with a whisk. Remove from the heat. Add eggs, one at a time, whisking after each addition. Add salt and pepper.

7. In a saucepan or deep fryer, heat the oil to 350°F (180°C). Do not overfill the saucepan or deep fryer.

8. One at a time, dip pieces of brain in the batter. Fry in the oil for about 5 minutes or until browned.

9. Remove them from the pan using a slotted spoon and place the calf brain popcorn on a wire rack. Add salt to taste.

10. Serve with pesto Parmesan mayo.

PAN-FRIED CHICKEN HEARTS +
BACON + GRAPES

If you have leftovers, they'll be perfect for your lunch at work the next day. That will really help you put your HEART into your work! Delicious with mashed potatoes.

Serves
3 amateur eaters or
2 competitive eaters
Prep time – 20 min
Cooking time – 20 min

1½ lbs (700 g) chicken hearts

6 slices of bacon, cut in matchsticks

2 onions, diced

2 tbsp (30 mL) vegetable oil (as needed)

2 garlic cloves, shoots removed, chopped

½ cup (125 mL) red grapes, halved

¼ cup (60 mL) balsamic vinegar

¼ cup (60 mL) chopped fresh parsley (optional)

Lemon zest (optional)

1. Remove the veins and arteries around the hearts, if this has not been done. Cut the hearts in half, place in a strainer and rinse thoroughly in cold water. Pat them with a paper towel to remove excess water. Set aside.

2. In a skillet, over medium-high heat, cook bacon. When fat starts to be released from the bacon, add onions. Cook until onions are golden brown. Set aside on a plate.

3. In the same skillet, over high heat, brown chicken hearts. If there is no bacon fat in the skillet, add vegetable oil.

4. Add garlic and grapes. Return onions and bacon to the skillet. Cook for 5 to 10 minutes or until hearts are cooked and nicely browned. Deglaze with balsamic vinegar. With a wooden spoon, scrape the bottom of the skillet to get all the browned bits. Continue to cook until liquid is reduced by half.

5. Add chopped parsley and lemon zest, if desired, and serve.

POULTRY LIVER PÂTÉ
+ PORT

I love making large quantities of this recipe: I freeze my small liver pâtés so I always have some on hand. You can replace the port with cognac or another liquor of your choice: have fun!

Makes
2 cups (500 mL)
Prep time – 30 min
Cooking time – 10 to 15 min
Refrigeration – 6 hours

6 tbsp (90 mL) butter, divided

1 cup (250 mL) finely chopped shallots

4 slices of bacon, finely chopped

1 lb (450 g) poultry or pork livers

½ cup (125 mL) port

½ cup (125 mL) heavy or whipping (35%) cream

1 tsp (5 mL) salt

¼ tsp (1 mL) ground white pepper

Bread slices or crackers

1. In a skillet, over low heat, melt 3 tbsp (45 mL) butter. Sauté shallots and bacon until shallots are transparent but not browned. Add livers and stir. Add port. Continue cooking for 10 minutes or until livers are cooked but still pink in the center.

2. In a blender or food processor, purée livers, the remaining 3 tbsp (45 mL) butter and the cream. Add salt and pepper, then blend again. Taste and adjust the seasoning as needed.

3. Spoon the mixture into ramekins or small containers with lids. Refrigerate for at least 6 hours before enjoying on bread or with crackers.

veal

Veal is the meat from a calf — the baby of a cow and a bull. The meat from this young animal is very popular in Europe (less so in North America), especially in France, the country that eats the most of it, closely followed by Italy. People enjoy veal for its subtle flavor as well as its tenderness. The thin fibers of the flesh offer a very tasty, smooth texture. It is also leaner than beef, with under 7.5% fat content.

Veal is divided into two categories: milk-fed and grain-fed. With milk-fed veal, calves are fed only with a specific milk that gives the meat a pale pinkish color. With grain-fed veal, calves receive feeding in two stages; they drink the same specific milk during their first few weeks of life, then they are fed grain (often corn). Their meat has a darker pink color.

Not surprisingly, veal cuts are fairly similar to beef cuts, even though a veal carcass weighs no more than 419 lbs (190 kg), less than half the weight of a cow weighs. However, veal is still cut in quarters. It offers a nice variety of cuts, including those that can be roasted, pan-fried or grilled and less tender muscles, such as the shank for osso buco or stewing cuts for blanquette of veal (classic French stew), which are also very popular.

This is a type of meat that is worth trying — it's VEALy good!

VEAL

FOREQUARTER VEAL CUTS

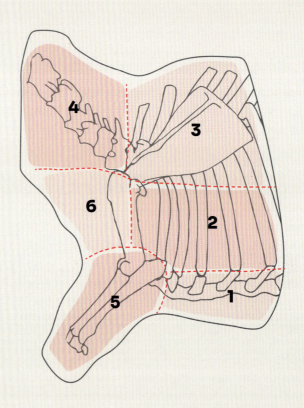

1 - BREAST (BRISKET) 4 - HEAD AND NECK
2 - CROSS RIB 5 - SHANK (FRONT)
3 - SHOULDER BLADE 6 - SHOULDER BONE

1 – THE BREAST (BRISKET)

This is a part of the animal that works hard so it takes longer to cook, though it's delicous. Referred to as the breast (rather than brisket in beef), it is not common to find it with the extension of the muscle found in the flank (as with beef). Often used for stews, it can also be sliced, ground or cut into stewing cubes. The boneless breast is very tasty on the smoker or the grill.

WHOLESALE CUT: BREAST	
Retail cut	Cooking method
Whole breast	Braise, simmer
Stew cubes	Simmer
Breast, sliced or pieces	Braise, simmer

2 – CROSS RIB

This group of muscles is heavily used by the animal as it moves around. Here we find, as in other animals, the shoulder petite tender (shoulder clod petite tender or *teres major*), which is incredibly tender and has a more pronounced flavor than filet mignon. The petite tender is excellent barbecued as well as raw. Similar to beef, the shoulder can be prepared as various cuts, such as shoulder cross rib roast, shoulder clod roast and sliced into chops. The short ribs cut from the cross rib work well for braising and are also delicious. After simmering, they become tender; you can even gnaw on the bones. In North America, certain shoulder muscles may be mechanicallly tenderized to make pieces for grilling, while this approach is almost nonexistent in Europe.

WHOLESALE CUT: CROSS RIB	
Retail cut	cooking method
Shoulder clod steak (ranch steak)	Grill, sauté
Short ribs	Braise, simmer, roast
Sliced short ribs	Grill, sauté
Stew cubes	Simmer
Shoulder scaloppini	Grill, sauté
Shoulder cross rib roast – *Individual muscle: pectoral*	Braise, simmer, roast – *Raw, grill, sauté*
Shoulder clod roast – *Individual muscle: shoulder petite tender*	Braise, simmer, roast – *Raw, grill, sauté*

3 – SHOULDER BLADE

A popular cut in Quebec, the shoulder blade contains the shoulder blade roast, where you will find the flat iron and shoulder blade eye. The flat iron includes a part for grilling and a part for stewing. The eye is mostly stewed so it will be tender and enjoyable to chew. The bottom blade is sometimes sold boneless, as a roast or cubed. The whole shoulder blade roast with the bone in includes the bottom and the top blade, which are separated by the scapula (which corresponds to the shoulder blade). Cuts from the shoulder blade are popular for cooking blanquette of veal (French veal stew) and other stews and braised dishes. You can also remove the first ribs of the blade to make shoulder-end chops, small chops that are becoming better known.

WHOLESALE CUT: SHOULDER BLADE	
Retail cut	**Cooking method**
Delmonico steak (first slice toward the rib)	Grill, sauté
Shoulder bottom blade roast - *Individual muscle: chuck flat/Denver steak*	Braise, simmer *Grill, sauté*
Shoulder top blade roast - *Individual muscle: flat iron* - *Indivdual muscle: shoulder blade eye*	Braise, simmer *Braise, grill, simmer, sauté* *Braise, simmer*
Bone-in shoulder blade roast (bottom + top + bone)	Braise, simmer

4 – HEAD AND NECK

Calves' head is not sold whole, but the cheeks and the tongue are available from the butcher. Although these are muscles, they are considered offal (see page 129). Of course, the head also contains the brain, which is protected by the skull (also called the cranial cavity). See section 6 on page 141 for details about meat cuts from the neck.

WHOLESALE CUT: HEAD	
Retail cut	**Cooking method**
Brain (blanched beforehand)	Fry, grill, sauté
Cheeks	Braise, simmer
Tongue	Braise, grill, simmer

5 – THE SHANK (FRONT)

Because these muscles are found at the front, they work harder when the animal is on the move. Like hindshank (back shank), foreshank is used for osso buco, even though it is less desirable and less meaty, as its bone also contains tasty marrow. Like hindshank, it is enjoyed as a whole shank, Frenched shank, called Thor's hammer, and more rarely as boneless shank.

WHOLESALE CUT: SHANK (FRONT)	
Retail cut	**Cooking method**
Stew cubes	Simmer
Shank center cut (whole)	Braise, simmer
Boneless shank (tied or not)	Braise, simmer
Rolled boneless shank	Braise, simmer
Osso buco (sliced)	Braise, simmer
Thor's hammer (Frenched shank)	Braise, simmer

6 – SHOULDER BONE AND NECK

These muscles from the neck and shoulder bone are usually deboned and cut in cubes to make veal blanquette, veal marengo and many other succulent dishes that require stewing cubes. Sometimes, the shoulder bone can be sliced perpendicular to the humerus (a marrow bone) to make slices like those used for osso buco. However, the result does not have the same texture, as this part is much less rich in collagen than meat from the shank. The humerus is a highly valued veal bone, including for making classic veal stock.

WHOLESALE CUT: SHOULDER + NECK	
Retail cut	**Cooking method**
Stew cubes	Braise, simmer
Shoulder bone (slice)	Braise, simmer

VEAL STEW + MUSTARD + MUSHROOMS

Serves
6 mildly hungry people or
3 ravenous people
Prep time – 30 min
Cooking time – 2 hours 15 min

Stew

⅓ cup (80 mL) vegetable oil

5 garlic cloves, shoots removed, halved

2 ¼ lbs (1 kg) veal stew cubes

½ tsp (2 mL) salt

½ tsp (2 mL) pepper

¼ tsp (1 mL) poultry seasoning (or rub, see page 100)

2 cups (500 mL) white wine

2 cups (500 mL) heavy or whipping (35%) cream

3 ⅓ cups (825 mL) veal stock

¾ cup (175 mL) Dijon mustard

2 cups (500 mL) white mushrooms, halved

2 tbsp (30 mL) all-purpose flour

¼ cup (60 mL) cornstarch

Cold water

Spices for the gravy

1 tsp (5 mL) garlic powder

1 tsp (5 mL) onion powder

½ tsp (2 mL) pepper

½ tsp (2 mL) poultry seasoning (or rub, see page 100)

½ tsp (2 mL) dried thyme

½ tsp (2 mL) dried rosemary

2 bay leaves

Hot cooked egg noodles

1. Stew. In a large saucepan, over high heat, heat oil and sauté garlic until golden brown. Remove from the saucepan and set aside.

2. In the same saucepan, sauté veal cubes with salt, pepper and poultry seasoning. When the cubes are nicely browned, deglaze with white wine, scraping the bottom with a wooden spoon to get all the brown bits. Simmer, until the liquid is reduced by half. Add cream, veal stock and Dijon mustard. Chop the reserved sautéed garlic and add it to the stew.

3. Spices for the gravy. In a bowl, combine all the ingredients. Add the mixture to the stew and stir well.

4. Simmer uncovered over low heat for 2 hours or until the meat is tender. About 20 minutes before the end of cooking, add mushrooms.

5. In a bowl, combine flour and cornstarch, then gradually add cold water until you get a consistency of thick glue. With a whisk, gradually add just enough of the mixture to the stew to thicken the gravy to the desired consistency (you may not need to add all the mixture).

6. Serve over egg noodles.

Note

I suggest using veal breast cubes, but any stewing meat will work for this recipe.

VEAL CROSS RIB ROAST + GARLIC + HERBS + SWEET-AND-SOUR SAUCE

Where the cross rib roast comes from: the cross rib

Serves
5 ordinary people or
3 outstanding people
Prep time – 45 min
Tempering – 20 min
Cooking time – 6 hours

Roast

1 veal bone-in cross rib shoulder roast (see Note), about 4½ lbs (2 kg)

Salt and pepper

2 to 3 tbsp (30 to 45 mL) vegetable oil

2 large onions, quartered

3 carrots, peeled and quartered

3 stalks celery, cut in thirds

6 garlic cloves, shoots removed, chopped

3 cups (750 mL) veal stock

8 baby potatoes

2 sprigs of rosemary

1 tbsp (15 mL) onion powder

3 sprigs of thyme (optional)

Sweet-and-sour sauce

¼ cup (60 mL) balsamic vinegar

½ cup (125 mL) veal stock

¼ cup (60 mL) honey

1. **Roast.** Unwrap the roast and let sit at room temperature on a wire rack for 20 minutes.
2. Preheat the oven to 275°F (135°C).
3. Salt and pepper the roast. In a Dutch oven or other oven-proof pot, over high heat, heat oil and sear roast on all sides until nicely browned.
4. Add onions, carrots, celery and garlic. Cook for 2 to 3 minutes. Deglaze with veal stock, scraping the bottom with a wooden spoon to get all the brown bits.
5. Add potatoes, rosemary and onion powder. Add thyme, if desired. Add salt and pepper.
6. Cover and bake for about 6 hours or until the meat is easily shredded with a fork.
7. **Sweet-and-sour sauce.** In a saucepan, over high heat, bring all the ingredients to a boil. With a whisk, stir the sauce constantly until it thickens and becomes syrupy. Set aside.
8. Pull the meat into large shreds and pull the bones apart to separate. Arrange the meat and vegetables on plates and drizzle with sweet-and-sour sauce.

Notes

The roast for this recipe is a cross rib from the shoulder with the bones cut off the meat separately, then wrapped around the roast and tied together with butcher's twine.

Keep the cooking stock from the roast. Strain it with a sieve and use it to make soup or gravy.

VEAL BLADE ROAST +
CITRUS + GREMOLATA

Where the blade comes from: the shoulder blade

For this recipe featuring citrus fruits, you will need two oranges, one pink grapefruit, one lemon and one lime. Garnish with kumquats if you have them.

Serves
6 timid eaters or
4 bold eaters
Prep time – 20 min
Cooking time – 3 hours

Veal blade

4½ lb (2 kg) bone-in veal shoulder blade
  roast (a thick slice, 4 inches/10 cm)
2 cups (500 mL) veal stock
¼ cup (60 mL) cubed butter
1 leek, white part only, cut in rings
1 onion, sliced
3 garlic cloves, shoots removed,
  chopped
3 tbsp (45 mL) honey
¼ cup (60 mL) balsamic vinegar
1 sprig of thyme
½ orange, sliced
½ pink grapefruit, sliced
Salt and pepper

Basil and citrus gremolata

Segments of ½ pink grapefruit
Segments of ½ orange
Zest and juice of 1 lemon
Zest of 1 lime
Zest of 1½ oranges
3 garlic cloves, shoots removed, finely
  chopped
1 cup (250 mL) finely chopped basil
½ cup (125 mL) finely chopped parsley
½ cup (125 mL) extra virgin olive oil
Salt and pepper

1. Preheat the oven to 325°F (160°C).
2. **Veal blade.** In a Dutch oven or other oven-proof large pot, combine all the ingredients. Cover and bake for 3 hours or until the meat is tender and is easily shredded with a fork.
3. **Basil and citrus gremolata.** Cut grapefruit and orange segments in thirds and place in a bowl. Add the remaining ingredients and stir.
4. Pull the meat apart into large chunks. Place the meat on the plates. Generously garnish with gremolata.

VEAL SHANK + OLIVES + PRESERVED LEMON

Where the shank comes from: the foreshank or hindshank

Pair the veal with grilled vegetables and couscous or roasted potatoes.

Serves
4 easy-going eaters or
2 high-octane eaters
Prep time – 30 min
Cooking time – 3 hours 20 min

Salt and pepper
4 slices of veal shank, about ¾ lb (350 g)
  each
¼ cup (60 mL) all-purpose flour
2 tbsp (30 mL) vegetable oil
3 tbsp (45 mL) butter
2 onions, diced
1 cup (250 mL) diced carrots
1 cup (250 mL) diced celery
2 cups (500 mL) veal stock
1 red bell pepper, diced
1 preserved lemon, sliced
½ cup (125 mL) pitted green olives
2 bay leaves
1 sprig of rosemary

For serving

Lemon zest

1. Preheat the oven to 250°F (125°C).
2. Salt and pepper the slices of veal to your taste, then coat evenly with flour.
3. In a large Dutch oven or other oven-proof large, shallow saucepan, over high heat, heat oil and butter. Sear the meat on all sides until nicely browned. Set aside on a plate.
4. In the same pot, cook onions, carrots and celery until soft. Deglaze with veal stock, scraping the bottom with a wooden spoon to get all the brown bits.
5. Return the veal slices to the pot. Add red pepper, preserved lemon slices, olives, bay leaves and rosemary.
6. Cover and bake for 3 hours, or until the meat is tender and easily comes off the bone. During cooking, stir occasionally so the veal doesn't stick to the bottom. If you need more liquid, add ¼ to 1 cup (60 to 250 mL) water.
7. Garnish with lemon zest to your taste, when ready to serve.

SAUSAGES + CAUL FAT + VARIATIONS

Where ground veal comes from: any meat cut or trimming

Here is a basic recipe for sausage meat that you can adapt to your taste.
You can put it into casing, but many people don't have a sausage stuffer at home,
so I decided to offer you a method that's accessible for everyone using caul fat.

Makes
about 2¼ lbs (1 kg) sausage meat
or 7 sausages
Prep time – 30 min to 1 hour

*It's best to weigh the ingredients
for this recipe to ensure the best
consistency.*

1 lb (450 g) VERY coarsely ground
  pork — ground only once (see Notes,
  page 94)
1 lb (450 g) ground veal fat — ground
  only once (see Notes, page 94)
4 tbsp + 2 tsp (70 g) cold water
0.6 oz (18 g) salt
1 tsp (2 g) pepper
¼ tsp (1 g) ground nutmeg
¼ tsp (1 g) ground ginger
Caul fat (see Notes, page 94)

1. In a large bowl, combine ground pork and ground veal. Set aside.
2. In a small bowl, combine water, salt, pepper, nutmeg and ginger.
3. Add the water and spices mixture to the meat. Mix well so the spices are spread evenly throughout the meat.
4. On a clean worktop, stretch out the caul fat. Cut rectangles 2 inches (5 cm) wide and the length desired for the sausages. Place about 5 ounces (150 g) sausage meat on each small rectangle, then roll. If the sausages are not compact enough or have holes, don't panic: just roll them in a second layer of caul fat.

Notes
You can have lots of fun with this recipe! Here are a few interesting variations:
- Replace the water with white or red wine, whiskey, apple juice, tomato juice, honey, maple syrup, beet juice, barbecue sauce, poutine gravy, etc.
- Use spices you like: fennel, basil, thyme, herbes de Provence, Italian seasoning, mustard, rosemary, dry ranch dressing mix, dry macaroni and cheese powder, etc.
- Add ingredients: dried or fresh fruit, vegetables, nuts, cheese, smoked meat, charcuterie, bacon, gherkins, olives, etc.
- Switch out the meat: 100% pork, lamb, beef, game, poultry, etc.

For cooking instructions, see Drumsticks + lollipop + mozzarella, page 188.

VEAL

CENTER AND HINDQUARTER
VEAL CUTS

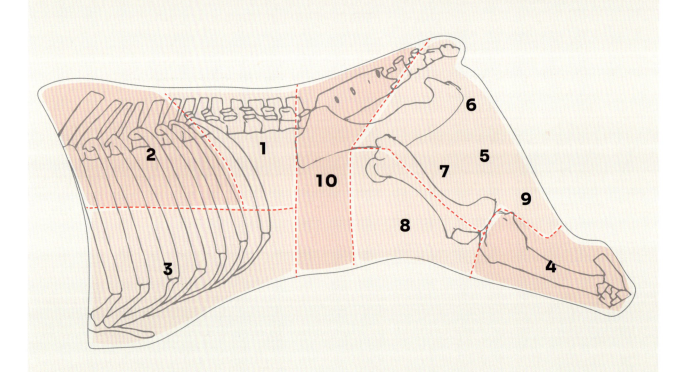

1 – LOIN

2 – RIB

3 – FLANK

4 – SHANK (HIND)

5 – BOTTOM (OUTSIDE) ROUND

6 – EYE OF ROUND

7 – TOP (INSIDE) ROUND

8 – SIRLOIN TIP

9 – HEEL OF ROUND

10 – SIRLOIN

1 – LOIN

The loin includes a large tenderloin end (where we get the T-bone steak) as well as a rib end (without tenderloin). The loin is scrumptious when cooked on the grill. It contains the tenderloin, which can be removed whole, with the head (butt) section, found in the sirloin (see page 159). A small, thin muscle, the tenderloin chain, is often removed from the whole tenderloin. Although very small compared to that found in beef, the chain still very tasty. Like the tenderloin, the strip (strip loin) is delicious sliced and grilled, and as a roast, but it is also excellent for tartare or tataki. As with beef, we sometimes see the tenderloin on the bone, with the meat removed from the vertebra (or not) — this is less common, but it's an attractive cut.

WHOLESALE CUT: LOIN	
Retail cut	**Cooking method**
Wing chop (13th rib only)	Grill, sauté
Loin chop (veal T-bone)	Grill, sauté
Loin chop without tenderloin	Grill, sauté
Tenderloin (center and tail) - *Individual muscle: chain (one part)*	Raw, grill, sauté *Grill*
Bone-in tenderloin	Grill (sliced), roast
Grenadin de veau (Veal tenderloin medallions wrapped in lard and tied)	Grill, roast, sauté
Strip roast (strip loin roast)	Roast
Loin roast (with tenderloin)	Roast
Bone-in loin roast (without tenderloin)	Roast
Tenderloin medallion	Raw, grill, sauté
Boneless loin steak or cutlet	Raw, grill, sauté

2 – THE RIB

This primal cut is used to make the very attractive rack of veal, with its white ribs showing. As Frenched rib chop, it is increasingly called veal tomahawk, and is equivalent to a beef rib steak. It can be deboned to make a roast or a steak but is less popular than rack of veal with the bones.

For connoisseurs: Toward the inside of the ribs, near the dorsal vertebrae, are found the kidneys, kidney fat and hanger steak, which is incredibly delicious. To enjoy the hanger fully, the central nerve must be removed, which makes two pieces.

WHOLESALE CUT: RIB	
Retail cut	**Cooking method**
Short ribs	Braise, simmer
Short ribs (sliced or grilling)	Grill, simmer, sauté
Rack of veal - *Individual muscle: complexus* - *Individual muscle: longissimus dorsi (loin)* - *Individual muscle: hanger (inside the rib cage)* - *Individual muscle: spinalis (ribeye cap)* - *Other: suet (inside the chest wall)*	Braise, grill, roast *Raw, grill, sauté* *Raw, grill, sauté* *Raw, grill, sauté* *Grill, sauté* *Melt*
Frenched rib chop (cowboy chop)	Grill, sauté
Ribeye chop (boneless)	Grill, sauté
Rib chops	Grill, roast, sauté
Back ribs	Braise, grill, simmer, roast
Rib roast	Braise, roast
Boneless ribeye roast	Braise, roast
Tomahawk	Grill, sauté

The meat cuts in this book are based on French-Canadian artisan butchery cuts, sometimes enriched with European French artisan butchery cuts, and they don't always match up exactly to US or Canadian English-language meat cuts and standard terminology. The appendix at the back of the book will help guide you, providing translations and possible alternate names for cuts, and you can visit your local butcher who may be able to help answer your questions.

3 – THE FLANK

The flank includes the part that will be removed to expose the ribs of the tomahawk. This is the belly of the animal, which is popular for stews. In Quebec, the flank is often deboned and rolled, and sometimes stuffed. In France, it is found sliced with its cartilage; this is called *tendron de veau*, which people like for its collagen content. Although it's delicious, flank is not one of the most popular cuts, but I think it is worth cooking. It includes part of the bavette (flap meat) and the flank muscle, the latter of which corresponds to beef flank steak, although obviously smaller.

WHOLESALE CUT: FLANK	
Retail cut	**Cooking method**
Bavette/flap meat (extension of the part in the sirloin)	Raw, grill, sauté
Frenched rack of short ribs	Braise, simmer, roast
Stew cubes	Simmer
Flank steak	Grill, simmer
Boneless rolled flank	Braise, grill, simmer, roast
Skirt	Raw, grill, sauté
Strips	Grill, sauté
Boneless breast (flank portion), rolled or not	Braise, grill (sometimes), simmer

4 – SHANK (HIND)

This highly prized cut is ideal for making osso buco, a typical Milanese dish that is popular around the world. Once the shank is sliced, you get a bone with a luscious marrow-filled hole in the middle. In fact, osso buco means "bone with a hole" in Italian! Meaty and tender, the high point of this dish is definitely enjoying the exquisite marrow. You can also find it boneless or as a whole shank, sometimes with the meat cleaned from the top of the bone (called Thor's hammer or Frenched). For a delicious result, it's important to cook it over low heat for a long time, until the meat falls off the bone.

WHOLESALE CUT: SHANK	
Retail cut	**Cooking method**
Center shank (whole)	Braise, simmer
Boneless shank	Braise, simmer
Osso buco (sliced)	Braise, simmer
Thor's hammer	Braise, simmer

5 – THE BOTTOM (OUTSIDE) ROUND

Containing lean muscles, the bottom (outside) round of the leg is mainly used for strips, stewing cubes and cutlets. It can also be made into roasts. Although not very tender, it is very tasty, and as a wholesale cut it corresponds to bottom (outside) round in beef. In North America, it is sometimes mechanically tenderized to make slices for grilling. The piece of meat is inserted between two rollers equipped with blades, which make tears in the meat fibers. This method makes it possible to turn tougher cuts into pieces for grilling and be sold at lower prices. Meat lovers don't really love these tenderized meats because the texture isn't the same.

WHOLESALE CUT: BOTTOM (OUTSIDE) ROUND	
Retail cut	**Cooking method**
Stew cubes	Braise, simmer
Cutlets	Grill, sauté
Strips	Grill, sauté
Outside leg roast	Braise, simmer, roast
Slices	Grill

6 – EYE OF ROUND

Because it's not very tender, eye of round is usually thinly sliced to make Chinese hot pot. Sometimes — particularly in North America — it can be tenderized mechanically and used to make medallions.

WHOLESALE CUT: EYE OF ROUND	
Retail cut	**Cooking method**
Eye of round cubes (tenderized or not)	Grill, sauté
Medallions	Grill, sauté
Eye of round roast	Simmer, roast
Eye of round slices (tenderized or not)	Grill, sauté
Fondue (thin slices)	Simmer, sauté

7 – THE TOP (INSIDE) ROUND

This leg cut is from the inside part of the thigh; here you find the same structure as in the top (inside) round (or *la noix*, in France) in beef (see page 51). Once the inside round cap and the bullet muscle have been removed, you get the stripped interior (containing the round and the inside tender). This piece is used mainly in scaloppini, a popular veal cut. You can also prepare the stripped interior as a roast, strips, cubes, tartare or tataki, and medallions. The bullet muscle and inside tender are delicious raw and grilled, whole or sliced.

WHOLESALE CUT: TOP (INSIDE) ROUND	
Retail cut	**Cooking method**
Cubes for kabobs	Grill
Stew cubes	Braise, simmer
Sandwich steaks (cubed steak)	Grill, sauté
Scaloppini	Grill, sauté
Top (inside) round - *Individual muscle: cap (stew cubes)* - *Individual muscle: inside tender* - *Individual muscle: bullet muscle*	Braise, raw, grill, simmer, roast, sauté *Braise, simmer* *Raw, fry, grill, sauté* *Raw, fry, grill, sauté*
Strips	Grill, sauté
Top (inside) round roast	Braise, simmer, roast
Top (inside) round slices/cutlets (tenderized or not)	Grill, sauté
Carpaccio	Raw
Tartare	Raw

8 – THE SIRLOIN TIP

As in beef cuts, there are three main parts: the round (center), the eye (side) and the cap. Although much smaller, the cap is delicious grilled, with a subtle, delicate flavor. The round makes an excellent veal roast or medallions. The eye can be used for scaloppini and sometimes for a roast (tenderized or not). The cap contains a more tender part of the muscle that can also be sliced into scallopini. What's left can be turned into stewing cubes or ground veal.

WHOLESALE CUT: THE SIRLOIN TIP	
Retail cut	**Cooking method**
Sandwich steak	Grill, sauté
Tenderized steak	Grill, sauté
Sirloin tip steak	Grill, sauté
Cubes for kabobs	Grill, sauté
Stew cubes (cap)	Braise, simmer
Scaloppini (eye/side and cap)	Grill, sauté
Strips	Grill, sauté
Medallions	Grill, sauté
Sirloin tip roast (round)	Roast
Fondue (thin slices)	Simmer, sauté

9 – THE HEEL OF THE ROUND

The heel of the round includes a group of muscles that are often cut to be used for stew cubes. There are also some more tender muscles that can be made into scaloppini. At the center of the heel is a small, thin, long muscle and a tendon that sticks out of one end, called the banana shank or red tail. In French, it's called the *carotte*, because its shape is like that vegetable, or it's called veal garlic clove (when sliced, the veins of collagen inside the muscle look like the inside of a clove of garlic). This muscle is often used in blanquettes and stews.

WHOLESALE CUT: HEEL	
Retail cut	**Cooking method**
Banana shank (red tail)	Braise, simmer
Stew cubes	Braise, simmer
Scaloppini	Grill, sauté

10 – THE SIRLOIN

Like with beef, the following cuts are made from veal sirloin: top sirloin cap (coulotte/picanha), mouse steak, top sirloin and a few small, less tender muscles, which are often turned into ground meat. The top sirloin contains a circular muscle, the top sirloin butt, center-cut, often called the top sirloin heart or top sirloin, cap off/removed. It can be made into roasts, steaks, scaloppini, cubes for grilling, and even strips. This piece also works well for tataki and tartare. The bottom sirloin contains the tri-tip (bottom sirloin tri-tip), part of the bavette (bottom sirloin flap) and tenderloin head (butt).

For connoisseurs: On the hip bone, toward the interior of the animal, between the sirloin and the sirloin tip, is found the oyster or spider steak. Comparable to the bavette, this small piece is tender but above all very high in flavor. The name spider comes from the fact that inside the muscle are eight small nerves connected to the center, like the eight legs of a spider. These must be removed for maximum enjoyment of this delicious and rare cut.

WHOLESALE CUT: SIRLOIN	
Retail cut	**Cooking method**
Bavette steak (bottom sirloin flap)	Raw, grill, sauté
Top sirloin butt, center-cut	Grill, roast, sauté
Stew cubes	Braise, simmer
Coulotte/picanha (whole)	Raw (if defatted), grill, roast
Coulotte/picanha (sliced)	Grill, sauté
Tenderloin head (butt) slices	Grill, sauté
Fondue (thin slices)	Fry, sauté
Tenderloin head (butt) medallions	Raw, grill, sauté
Boneless sirloin roast	Roast
Tenderloin head (butt), roast	Grill, roast
Filet medallions	Grill, sauté
Sirloin steak (whole) - *Individual muscle: oyster or spider (in the groin)* - *Individual muscle: faux araignée (false spider)* - *Individual muscle: mouse* - *Individual muscle: tri-tip*	Grill, roast (if sliced thick) *Grill, sauté* *Simmer* *Raw, grill, sauté* *Raw, grill, roast, sauté*
Boneless sirloin steak	Raw (if defatted), grill, sauté
Boneless sirloin steak (without tenderloin)	Grill, roast (if sliced thick)

VEAL LOIN CHOPS + COWBOY BUTTER + HERBED BABY POTATOES

160

Indulge in this amazing cowboy butter for dipping your meat and baby potatoes. If you're on a diet, keep your distance!

Serves – 4 civilized people or 2 to 3 wild people
Prep time – 30 min   **Tempering** – 20 to 30 min   **Cooking time** – 1 hour   **Resting time** – 5 to 10 min

Loin chops

4 veal loin chops, 1½ inches (4 cm) thick
Salt

Herbed baby potatoes

Salt
20 medium-sized baby potatoes
Fresh herbs (bay leaf, rosemary, thyme, sage) of your choice
3 garlic cloves, shoots removed, sliced finely
Vegetable oil
Pepper

Cowboy butter

2 shallots, finely chopped
2 garlic cloves, shoots removed, finely chopped
1 tsp (5 mL) dried thyme
2 tbsp (30 mL) smoked paprika
1 tbsp (15 mL) hot pepper flakes
1 tbsp (15 mL) Worcestershire sauce
1 tbsp (15 mL) Dijon mustard
¼ cup (60 mL) chopped parsley
¼ cup (60 mL) finely sliced green onions
1 cup (250 mL) butter

1. **Loin chops.** Unwrap the veal chops and let sit at room temperature on a wire rack for 20 to 30 minutes.

2. Preheat the barbecue to high on just one side of the grill; for a charcoal grill, use a charcoal chimney starter to get glowing coals and place it at one end of the grill.

3. **Herbed baby potatoes.** In a saucepan filled with salted water, boil potatoes for 10 to 15 minutes or until tender. Drain.

4. Make a deep cut, lengthwise, in each potato (be careful not to cut it in half). Insert fresh herbs and one or two slices of garlic in the cavities. Place on a parchment paper-lined baking sheet. Oil generously and add salt and pepper to your taste.

5. Cook over indirect heat for 30 minutes or until potatoes are golden. Turn over potatoes a few times during cooking, if needed.

6. **Cowboy butter.** In a bowl, combine all the ingredients except butter. In a saucepan, over high heat, melt butter. Add the remaining ingredients and stir. When butter starts to foam, remove from the heat and set aside.

7. Evenly salt the veal chops to your taste. Sear on the grill, over direct heat or place directly in the coals, until nicely browned, turning halfway through cooking. If pieces of charcoal stick to the meat, remove them with tongs.

8. Move the chops over indirect heat to continue cooking until the internal temperature reaches 133°F (56°C) and they are pink in the center for rare or to your desired doneness.

9. Set aside on a plate and let rest, covered with foil, for 5 to 10 minutes.

10. Place a few potatoes and one chop on each plate, drizzle with cowboy butter and serve.

> **Note**
> If you prefer to use the stove and oven: preheat the oven to 375°F (190°C). In a large oven-proof skillet, over high heat, heat oil and sear the veal chops on both sides. Transfer the skillet to the oven and bake until the internal temperature reaches 133°F (56°C).

VEAL RIB CHOPS + ROASTED FENNEL + LEMON VINAIGRETTE

Where the chops come from: the rib

Serves
2 fearful eaters or
1 fearless eater
Prep time – 30 min
Tempering – 30 min
Cooking time – 45 min
Resting time – 5 to 10 min

Veal chops

2 Frenched veal rib chops, 1½ inches
  (4 cm) thick
Salt

Lemon vinaigrette

½ cup (125 mL) vegetable oil
¼ cup (60 mL) lemon juice
Zest of 1 lemon
1 tbsp (15 mL) Dijon mustard
Salt and pepper

Roasted fennel

1 fennel bulb, cut in quarters (keep the
  leaves for presentation)
3 shallots, cut in half lengthwise
2 tbsp (30 mL) vegetable oil
Salt and pepper
2 tbsp (30 mL) butter
4 garlic cloves, shoots removed, halved
1 sprig of thyme

1. Veal chops. Unwrap the veal chops and let sit at room temperature on a wire rack for 30 minutes.

2. Lemon vinaigrette. Place all the ingredients in a Mason jar. Close the jar and shake vigorously to emulsify until smooth. Set aside.

3. Preheat the barbecue to high on just one side of the grill; for a charcoal grill, use a charcoal chimney starter to get glowing coals and place it at one end of the grill.

4. Roasted fennel. In a large bowl, combine fennel, shallots and oil. Add salt and pepper to your taste and stir well. Cook on the grill over direct heat until the vegetables are nicely browned, turning them halfway through cooking. Transfer the vegetables to a cast-iron or other grill-safe skillet and continue cooking over indirect heat. Add butter, garlic and thyme. Let butter foam until lightly browned. When butter is brown, stir, and remove the skillet from the heat.

5. Evenly salt the meat to your taste. Place the veal chops on the grill over direct heat or in the coals and cook until nicely browned, turning them halfway through cooking. Move to indirect heat and continue cooking until the internal temperature reaches 135°F (57°C) and they are pink in the center for rare or to desired doneness.

6. Set on a wire rack and let rest 5 to 10 minutes. The chops should reach 140°F (60°C). Yes, the temperature rises during the resting stage!

7. Place one chop, some grilled vegetables and vinaigrette on each plate, and serve.

Note

Extra Lemon Vinaigrette can be stored in the jar in the fridge for up to 1 week. Use it on salads, grilled veggies, potatoes and on pork, veal or chicken.

Note

If you prefer to use the stove and oven: preheat oven to 375°F (190°C). In a large oven-proof skillet, over high heat, heat the oil and sear the veal chops on both sides. Transfer skillet to the oven and bake until the internal temperature reaches 135°F (57°C).

OSSO BUCO + REMIX + PUTTANESCA

Serves
4 nice people
or 2 impressive people
Prep time – 30 min
Cooking time – 2 hours 15 min

Osso buco

4 slices veal shank (osso buco-style),
  2 inches (5 cm) thick
Salt
¼ cup (60 mL) all-purpose flour
3 tbsp (45 mL) vegetable oil

Puttanesca sauce

8 garlic cloves, shoots removed, finely
  chopped
2 onions, finely chopped
2 stalks celery, diced
2 carrots, diced
1 cup (250 mL) dry white wine
4 cups (1 L) puréed tomatoes
⅓ cup (80 mL) black olives, drained
  and halved
2 to 3 anchovy fillets, sliced finely
  (optional)
2 tbsp (30 mL) capers, drained
1 tbsp (15 mL) dried oregano

To serve

Hot cooked pasta

1. Preheat the oven to 350°F (180°C).

2. Osso buco. Dry the veal with a paper towel. Salt the meat to taste and coat with flour.

3. In a Dutch oven or oven-proof large, deep skillet, over medium-high heat, heat oil and sear the veal slices until nicely browned on all sides. Set aside on a plate.

4. Puttanesca sauce. In the same pot, over medium heat, sauté garlic, onions, celery and carrots for 5 minutes. Deglaze with white wine, scraping the bottom with a wooden spoon to get all the brown bits. Add puréed tomatoes, olives, anchovies (if using), capers and oregano. Stir well.

5. Return the veal slices to the pot. Cover and bake for 2 hours or until the meat comes easily off the bone. Serve on a bed of pasta.

Notes

Add a piece of Parmesan cheese rind to the sauce with the puréed tomatoes to enhance the umami flavor of the sauce.

You can also add large caper berries, cut in half, for the last 5 minutes of cooking for a salty, briny punch.

VEAL TARTARE +
HASH BROWNS + HERBS

Where the top round comes from: the top (inside) leg

Serves
2 serene people
or 1 flamboyant person
Prep time – 30 min
Refrigeration – 30 min

Turmeric aioli

¼ cup (60 mL) mayonnaise

1 tsp (5 mL) ground turmeric

1 garlic clove, shoot removed, finely
  chopped

Veal tartare

1 lb (450 g) veal leg top (inside) round,
  cut in small cubes

2 tbsp (30 mL) chopped fresh parsley

2 tbsp (30 mL) chopped fresh chives

1 tbsp (15 mL) chopped fresh tarragon

1 tbsp (15 mL) Dijon mustard

1 tbsp (15 mL) mayonnaise

½ shallot, chopped finely

For garnish

2 store-bought hash browns, cooked
  and cooled

Caper pearls (see recipe, page 69)

Pickled shallots (see recipe, page 43)

Small sour pickles, sliced finely

Cucumber ribbons

1. Place a large bowl in the fridge for 30 minutes.
2. Turmeric aioli. In a bowl, combine all the ingredients. Cover and refrigerate.
3. Veal tartare. In the large cold bowl, combine all the ingredients well.
4. Place one hash brown on each plate and place the veal tartare on top. Arrange the caper pearls, pickled shallots, pickles and cucumber ribbons (see photo) on the veal. End with a dab of turmeric aioli and serve.

Note

Because the meat is eaten raw, be sure that the meat you purchase is not mechanically tenderized.

VEAL SIRLOIN TIP ROAST +
MISO + BEER + ORANGE

Where the roast comes from: the sirloin tip

Serves
4 regular eaters or
3 aggressive eaters
Prep time – 25 min
Cooking time – 1 hour 50 min
Resting time – 15 min

Miso beer sauce

1 cup (250 mL) beer
¼ cup (60 mL) miso
¼ cup (60 mL) soy sauce
2 tbsp (30 mL) mirin
1 tbsp (15 mL) sesame oil

Roast

¼ cup (60 mL) vegetable oil
1 veal sirloin tip roast, about 4½ lbs
  (2 kg)
2 onions, cut in ½-inch (1 cm) slices
1 orange, sliced

1. Preheat the oven to 250ºF (125ºC).

2. **Miso beer sauce.** Combine all the ingredients. Set aside.

3. **Roast.** In a Dutch oven or other oven-proof large pot, over high heat, heat oil until it starts to smoke. Sear the roast on all sides. Transfer to a plate.

4. Place onion slices in the pot and set the roast on top. Pour the sauce into the pot. Arrange a few orange slices on and around the roast (keep a few slices for serving).

5. Insert an oven-safe meat thermometer in the center of the meat. Bake, uncovered, for about 1 hour and 45 minutes, or until the internal temperature reaches 131ºF (55ºC) for rare or until desired doneness.

6. Remove the roast from the oven. Cover with foil and let rest for 15 minutes. The roast should have an internal temperature of 140ºF (60ºC) (yes, it rises during resting!).

7. Finely slice the roast and arrange on the plates. Garnish with cooking juices and orange slices.

VEAL TENDERLOIN + ROASTED PEPPERS + OLIVES + PROSCIUTTO

Serves
4 good eaters or
3 exceptional eaters
Prep time – 25 min
Tempering – 15 min
Cooking time – 20 min
Resting time – 5 to 10 min

Veal medallions

4 veal tenderloin medallions, 1½ inches (4 cm) thick
Salt
¼ cup (60 mL) vegetable oil

Roasted pepper and olive salsa

2 roasted red bell peppers, finely diced (see Notes)
1 onion, finely diced
4 plum (Roma) tomatoes, finely diced
¼ cup (60 mL) extra virgin olive oil
½ cup (125 mL) sliced black olives, drained
Zest and juice of 1 lemon
2 garlic cloves, shoots removed, finely chopped
Chopped fresh basil
Salt and pepper

Prosciutto chips

4 slices of prosciutto

1. Preheat the oven to 350ºF (180ºC). Line a baking sheet with parchment paper.

2. **Veal medallions.** Unwrap the veal medallions and let sit at room temperature on a wire rack for 15 minutes.

3. **Roasted pepper and olive salsa.** In a bowl, combine all the ingredients. Cover and refrigerate.

4. **Prosciutto chips.** Spread prosciutto slices in a single layer on prepared baking sheet. Bake for about 15 minutes, or until crispy. Set aside.

5. Lightly and evenly salt the veal to your taste (there will be salty ingredients served with it). In a skillet, over medium-high heat, heat oil and sear the veal on all sides until the internal temperature reaches 135ºF (57ºC) and the meat is pink in the center for rare (after searing, transfer the skillet to the oven and continue cooking the meat, if needed). Let rest for 5 to 10 minutes.

6. Arrange the veal medallions on the plates and garnish with roasted pepper and olive salsa. Crumble a prosciutto chip over each medallion and serve.

Notes

You can use store-bought jarred roasted peppers or roast them yourself in the oven or over the coals (don't forget to let them cool before removing the skin).

By the way, this recipe is great on the barbecue! Preheat the barbecue to high on just one side of the grill; for a charcoal grill, use a charcoal chimney starter to get glowing coals and place it on one side of the grill. Cook the prosciutto over indirect heat and sear the veal medallions over direct heat.

VEAL SIRLOIN ROAST + CHORIZO + PRUNES + BEER

Serves
4 sensible people or
3 eccentric people
Prep time – 40 min
Cooking time – 1 hour
Resting time – 15 min

Roast

Salt

1 veal top sirloin butt, center-cut roast, about 2¼ lbs (1 kg), not tied

Caul fat (see Notes, page 94)

5 prunes

5 thin slices of cured chorizo (your choice of spicy or mild)

3 tbsp (45 mL) vegetable oil

Prune and beer sauce

2 onions, diced

2 garlic cloves, shoots removed, chopped

4 oz (125 g) cured chorizo, diced (the same type you used for the roast)

2 cups (500 mL) strong beer

2 cups (500 mL) veal stock

12 prunes

1 sprig of rosemary

Equipment

Butcher's twine

1. Preheat the oven to 275°F (135°C).

2. **Roast.** Evenly salt the meat to your taste. Wrap in caul fat. Place the prunes and chorizo slices on top. Tie (see photo) once along the length, then at regular intervals along the width. Finish with a shoelace knot (see page 126).

3. In a Dutch oven or other oven-proof large pot, over medium-high heat, heat the oil. Sear the roast on all sides until nicely browned. Set aside on a plate.

4. **Prune and beer sauce.** In the pot, sauté onions, garlic and diced chorizo for 2 to 3 minutes. Deglaze with beer, scraping the bottom with a wooden spoon to get all the browned bits. Boil until the liquid is reduced by half. Add veal stock, prunes and rosemary, and stir. Return the roast to the pot.

5. Bake uncovered for 30 to 40 minutes, or until the internal temperature reaches 120°F (50°C) for very rare or to your desired doneness. Remove the roast from the cocotte and wrap in foil. Let rest 15 minutes.

6. With a fork, crush the prunes in the sauce.

7. Serve the roast sliced with the sauce.

Note

The top sirloin butt, center-cut roast is also called the top sirloin heart or top sirloin, cap off (or removed).

POULTRY

Poultry includes several species of birds: quail, partridge, guinea fowl, duck, pheasant, goose, turkey, Cornish hen, pigeon and, obviously, chicken. The ever-popular chicken is the second most commonly eaten meat in the world, just behind pork. Chicken is versatile and can be enjoyed whole or cut up, and you can make a nice stock with the carcass and even the feet.

Capon is a male chicken that has been castrated and specially raised for greater tenderness. It also weighs more than a regular chicken. Its female equivalent is a poularde in French. However, in North America, "capon" is generally used to describe a large chicken, as the castration of poultry is not commonly done — it is an invasive and painful procedure.

Very popular in the restaurant trade, duck can be considered as both poultry and feathered game (see page 205). Its high iron content (compared to other birds) as well as its healthier fat make it an excellent choice in terms of nutritional value. If it has been force-fed, its breast is called magret. And without force feeding? Duck breast!

Turkey tends to be eaten at specific times of year, especially at Thanksgiving and Christmas. Very lean, it is also popular for its nutritional value.

Partridge, pheasant, guinea fowl and quail are also lean varieties of poultry but are still flavorful. Butchers often recommend cooking them with fat or lardons to keep them from drying out.

Poultry must be thoroughly cooked, with its safe internal cooking temperature being 165°F (74°C) based on government regulations. One exception: duck magret or breast, which is excellent rare.

Poultry is delicious and so versatile. Best of CLUCK!

POULTRY

POULTRY CUTS

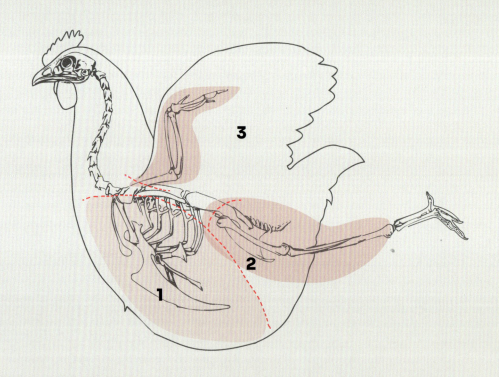

1 – BREAST
2 – LEG
3 – WING

WHOLE POULTRY

While poultry is well known and loved when roasted whole, you can also remove the back-bone and flatten the bird, which is called spatchcocking. This makes it easier to grill, because it requires a shorter cooking time. Whole poultry can also be found at stores boneless, semi-boneless and even stuffed. Half chickens (with half a breast and one leg) are commonly sold. You can find the feet with some whole poultry or ask your butcher for them. Because they are very high in collagen, they are choice pieces for stocks and sauces.

WHOLESALE CUT: WHOLE POULTRY	
Retail cut	**Cooking method**
With bone and skin	Braise, fry, grill, simmer, roast
Half chicken	Braise, fry, grill, simmer, roast
Boneless (with or without skin) and tied	Braise, fry, grill, simmer, roast
Boneless roast whole chicken, not tied	Braise, fry, grill, simmer, roast
Boneless and stuffed	Braise, fry, grill, simmer, roast
Spatchcocked	Braise, fry, grill, simmer, roast
Chicken feet	Braise, fry, grill, simmer, roast

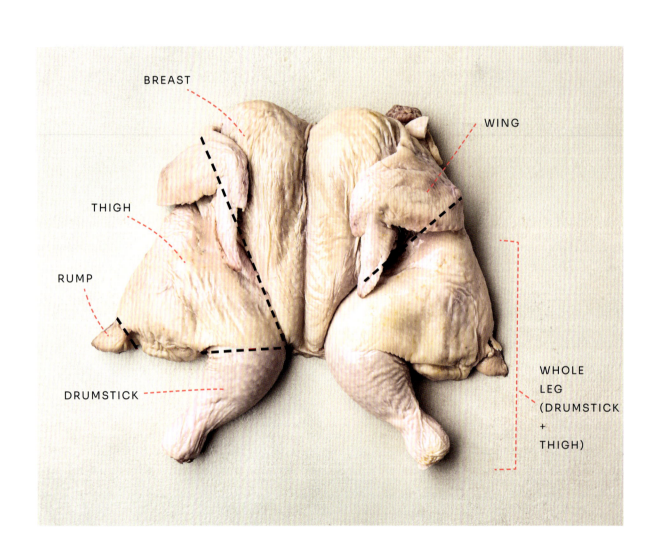

BREAST

WING

THIGH

RUMP

DRUMSTICK

WHOLE
LEG
(DRUMSTICK
+
THIGH)

1 – BREAST

The breast contains two half breasts: the right and the left. In some places, a half breast may be called a "chicken breast" but that's just a short form. You can buy half breasts with or without the bones and with or without skin. Rarely, butchers prepare what are known as breast chop: the bone is kept in and the piece is sliced perpendicularly, giving it the appearance of a chop. In each breast are two filets, on the carcass side, that contain a small central nerve. When the breast is kept whole on its rib cage, this is called chicken chest or whole breast on the bone. The breast is very popular and can be used in many ways. If it is boneless, it can be made into cubes, strips, tournedos and thinly sliced into scaloppini or cutlets; it can also be stuffed.

WHOLESALE CUT: BREAST	
Retail cut	**Cooking method**
Breast chop (slice of breast with bone in)	Grill, sauté
Kabob cubes	Grill, sauté
Stew cubes	Braise, grill, simmer
Boneless breast (with or without skin)	Braise, fry, grill, simmer, roast
Split breast (with bone and skin)	Braise, fry, grill, simmer, roast
Scaloppini or cutlets	Grill, sauté
Strips	Grill, sauté
Duck breast (boneless)	Grill, roast
Duck crown (with bone)	Grill, roast
Chicken paupiettes	Braise, simmer, roast
Chicken chest (whole breast/double on the bone) on the bone - *Individual muscle: filet (1 filet per half breast)*	Braise, fry, grill, simmer, roast *Grill, sauté*
Whole breast (double) with bone in, without back	Braise, fry, grill, simmer, roast
Stuffed breast	Braise, grill, roast
Boneless breast roast (with or without skin)	Braise, roast
Breast tournedos	Grill, simmer, roast
Thin breast slices for fondue	Fry, simmer, sauté

2 – LEG

The leg contains two main cuts, considered the dark meat for poultry: the drumstick and the thigh. The drumstick is made up of the metatarsal bone (shank) with its epiphysis, the bulbous wide part, at each end. This more affordable cut is often sold with the bones and skin, but it is also available boneless or semi-boneless and stuffed. A lollipop drumstick is made by removing the meat from part of the metatarsal and, sometimes, removing the epiphysis. The bone then looks like a lollipop stick! Turkey and chicken drumsticks are increasingly popular cut into sections. When they are sliced this way, some merchants call them turkey or chicken osso buco. Very tender, they can be prepared in various ways: boneless and skinless, with skin and bones, rolled, stuffed and even cut into scaloppini or cutlets.

For connoisseurs: Embedded in the groove of the coccyx, near the rump (the tail area on poultry), is found a small, very tender muscle that is sometimes mistaken for the oyster. It is hard to find in the US and Canada, but in France they call it *faux sot-l'y-laisse*. The real oyster is found along the spine at the thigh. It has a long, thin shape, and it is delicious!

CARNIVORE

WHOLESALE CUT: LEG (DRUMSTICK + THIGH)	
Retail cut	**Cooking method**
Bone-in leg quarter (with or without skin)	Braise, fry, grill, simmer, roast
- *Individual muscle: faux sot-l'y-laisse (in the hollow of the thigh)*	*Grill, sauté*
- *Individual muscle: oyster (along the spine)*	*Grill, sauté*
Boneless leg (with or without skin)	Braise, fry, grill, simmer, roast
Stuffed boneless leg (with or without skin)	Braise, fry, grill, simmer, roast
Bone-in, skin-on leg	Braise, fry, grill, simmer, roast
Boneless, skinless leg	Braise, fry, grill, simmer, roast
Scaloppini/cutlets	Grill, sauté
Bone-in thigh (with skin or skinless)	Braise, fry, grill, simmer, roast
Boneless thigh (with skin or skinless)	Braise, fry, grill, simmer, roast
Strips	Grill, sauté
Drumstick with skin	Braise, fry, grill, simmer, roast
Boneless drumstick with skin	Braise, fry, grill, simmer, roast
Stuffed boneless drumstick	Braise, fry, grill, simmer, roast
Butterflied drumstick (with the bone open like a butterfly)	Braise, fry, grill, simmer, roast
Frenched (lollipop) drumstick	Braise, fry, grill, simmer, roast
Frenched (lollipop) drumstick, stuffed	Braise, fry, grill, simmer, roast
Skinless drumstick	Braise, fry, grill, simmer, roast
Sliced drumstick (osso buco style)	Braise, fry, grill, simmer
Rolled stuffed thigh	Braise, fry, grill, roast

3 – WING

Whole wings have three parts: the tip, the flat and the drumette. Sometimes, the tip is removed, as it has very little meat. When the flat and the drumette are separated, this is called split wings; you will often find them in restaurants and in the frozen foods section of the grocery store. For those who like trying new things, the wing can be completely deboned and stuffed. Wings are mainly enjoyed barbecued or fried in North America. In Europe, they tend to be used to make stock and sauces.

For connoisseurs: In winged poultry, there is a small muscle attached to the rib cage which connects the wing to the humerus and becomes developed with wing flapping. While butchers don't usually sell this muscle separately, if you're cutting up whole poultry, chickens or wild turkey for example, it's worth carving off the bone to separate it out to cook up and enjoy this tender and delicious muscle that looks like a small nugget.

WHOLESALE CUT: WING	
Retail cut	**Cooking method**
Whole wings with bone and skin - *Individual muscle: wing candy* - *Individual muscle: flat* - *Individual muscle: drumettes* - *Individual muscle: wing tip*	Fry, grill, simmer, roast, sauté *Grill, sauté* *Fry, grill, simmer, roast, sauté* *Braise, fry, grill, simmer, roast* *Simmer*
Whole wings, boneless	Fry, grill, simmer, roast, sauté
Whole wings, boneless and stuffed	Fry, grill, simmer, roast, sauté
Whole wings, skinless	Fry, grill, simmer, roast, sauté
Split wings, flats and drumettes	Fry, grill, simmer, roast, sauté

The meat cuts in this book are based on French-Canadian artisan butchery cuts, sometimes enriched with European French artisan butchery cuts, and they don't always match up exactly to US or Canadian English-language meat cuts and standard terminology. The appendix at the back of the book will help guide you, providing translations and possible alternate names for cuts, and you can visit your local butcher who may be able to help answer your questions.

CORDON BLEU + POTATO CHIPS + ONION DIP

Where the cut comes from: breast

Serves
6 reasonable eaters or
4 belligerent eaters
Prep time – 25 min
Refrigeration – 6 to 12 hours
Cooking time – 10 min
(or 30 to 45 min in the oven)

Onion dip

½ cup (125 mL) sour cream

½ cup (125 mL) mayonnaise

1 small to medium sweet onion, grated

1 small garlic clove, shoot removed,
  finely chopped

1 tbsp (15 mL) onion powder

Salt and pepper

Chicken cordon bleu

4 slices chicken breast scaloppini
  (see Notes)

8 thin slices of ham

4 mozzarella cheese strings

Cooking oil

Potato chip coating

3 eggs

Salt and pepper

1 cup (250 mL) all-purpose flour

1 cup (250 mL) plain kettle potato chips,
  coarsely crushed

1 cup (250 mL) panko crumbs

1. Onion dip. In a bowl, combine all the ingredients. Cover and refrigerate (the dip is even better when made ahead).

2. Chicken cordon bleu. On a clean worktop, place the scaloppini flat in a single layer. In the middle of each piece, place 2 slices of ham and 1 cheese string.

3. Fold the ends of the breast toward the center and roll tightly, like a burrito. Wrap each stuffed breast in plastic wrap, making a tight sausage shape. Refrigerate for 6 to 12 hours.

4. In a saucepan or deep fryer, heat enough oil to immerse the stuffed rolls for deep-frying to 350°F (180°C).

5. Potato chip coating. In a bowl, beat eggs (within an inch of their lives!); add salt and pepper to your taste. In a second bowl, place flour and, in a third bowl, combine potato chips and panko crumbs.

6. Unwrap the stuffed chicken breasts and dip them in flour; shake to remove the excess. Dip in the beaten eggs, then in the potato chip coating. Do this dipping sequence two or three times, to your taste.

7. Fry the cordons bleus in oil for about 10 minutes or until golden and cooked all the way through, and the internal temperature of the chicken reaches 165°F (74°C). Serve with onion dip.

Notes

Ask your butcher to prepare the chicken breast scaloppini fairly thin, so you can stuff them and roll them. This is a must-try recipe . . . even in the oven!

Place the cordons bleus on a baking sheet lined with parchment paper and bake at 375°F (190°C) for 30 to 45 minutes or until the internal temperature reaches 165°F (74°C).

Notes
Are the wings split or whole? Adjust the cooking time accordingly!

You can cook chicken on a wire rack placed on a baking sheet lined with parchment paper in a preheated 425°F (220°C) oven.

CHICKEN WINGS + BUFFALO SAUCE + BLUE CHEESE SAUCE

Where the cut comes from: the wings

This is a recipe I love eating in my living room while watching TV . . . but it is delicious in the kitchen as well!

Serves
4 Sunday eaters or
2 Olympic eaters
Prep time – 25 min
Cooking time – 45 min

Chicken wings

¼ cup (60 mL) packed brown sugar

2 tbsp (30 mL) paprika

1 tbsp (15 mL) garlic powder

1 tbsp (15 mL) onion powder

2 tsp (10 mL) salt

12 chicken wings, split (24 pieces total; see Notes)

Radish slices (for serving)

Cucumber slices (for serving)

Blue cheese sauce

1 cup (250 mL) mayonnaise

¼ cup (60 mL) blue cheese

1 tsp (5 mL) honey

Salt and pepper

Buffalo sauce

¼ cup (60 mL) butter

½ cup (125 mL) Louisiana-style hot sauce

2 tbsp (30 mL) packed brown sugar or granulated sugar

1 tbsp (15 mL) apple cider vinegar

Equipment

Smoking wood chips

1. **Chicken wings.** In a small sealable container, place the brown sugar, paprika, garlic powder, onion powder and salt. Tightly close the container and shake vigorously to blend the seasonings well.

2. In a large bowl, place the wings and add the desired amount of seasoning. Cover the wings well. Refrigerate. (Store any extra seasoning for up to 3 months.)

3. **Blue cheese sauce.** In a food processor or blender, blend all the sauce ingredients until smooth. Taste and adjust seasoning as needed. Cover and refrigerate.

4. For a charcoal grill, use a charcoal chimney starter to get glowing coals and place it at one end of the grill and add your choice of smoking wood.

5. **Buffalo sauce.** In a saucepan, over medium-high heat, bring all the ingredients to a boil. Remove from the heat and set aside.

6. Place the chicken wings on the grill over indirect heat at about 350°F (180°C) and smoke them until the internal temperature reaches 156°F (68°C). Add charcoal to increase the barbecue temperature to 450°F to 500°F (230°C to 260°C) and grill the wings over direct heat and brown them until the internal temperature reaches 165°F (74°C).

7. Place the wings in a large bowl. Add Buffalo sauce to taste. Stir well to coat.

8. Serve the wings with blue cheese sauce and garnish with radish and cucumber slices.

DRUMSTICKS + LOLLIPOP + MOZZARELLA

Serves
4 average eaters or
2 above-average eaters
Prep time – 45 min
Cooking time – 45 min
Resting time – 5 to 10 min

4 chicken drumsticks (see Note)

2 Italian sausages, casings removed, or 14 oz (400 g) sausage meat

(see recipe, page 151)

Four 1¼-inch (3 cm) cubes mozzarella cheese

4 slices of bacon

Salt

Equipment

Butcher's twine

1. Preheat the oven to 350°F (180°C) or the smoker to indirect heat at 250°F (125°C).
2. Gently remove skin from the chicken drumsticks. Trim the skin into large rectangles and set aside.
3. Clean bones so there's no meat on them. To do this, remove the periosteum, the fibrous layer that separates the bone from the meat (see photo). Set aside.
4. Divide the sausage meat into 4 equal portions and shape into balls. Insert a cheese cube in each ball.
5. Stick a drumstick bone into each ball. Cover the sausage balls with the chicken meat from the drumstick.
6. Make an incision in the center of each of the reserved chicken skins. Push a drumstick bone through the hole and completely cover the stuffed drumstick with the skin. Wrap with a slice of bacon, tie some twine around the bacon and tighten.
7. Evenly salt the drumsticks to your taste. Bake or smoke until the internal temperature reaches 160°F (71°C).
8. Set aside on a plate and let rest for 5 to 10 minutes.
9. Enjoy as is or on pasta with marinara or pesto sauce.

Note

If possible, remove the epiphyses (the two balls at the end of the bone) or ask your butcher to do it for you. If these are removed, the lollipop look will be more obvious, but it's optional.

Note

To cook on the barbecue: preheat the barbecue to high; for a charcoal grill, use a charcoal chimney starter to get glowing coals. Boil water in a saucepan and cook the potatoes. Drain, then flatten them with a glass. Oil the potatoes and grill them over direct heat until nicely browned. For thighs, place them on the grill over direct heat.

CHICKEN THIGHS +
FLATTENED POTATO SALAD

Where the cut comes from: the leg

Serves
5 to 6 small eaters or
2 to 4 big eaters
Prep time – 1 hour
Cooking time – 1 hour
Resting time – 5 min

Potato salad

5 cups (1.25 L) baby potatoes
¼ cup (60 mL) vegetable oil
Salt and pepper
1 cup (250 mL) diced cucumber
½ cup (125 mL) finely chopped green
  onions
⅓ cup (75 mL) fresh dill, chopped finely
3 radishes, sliced finely
1 cup (250 mL) finely chopped leeks,
  white and light green parts
½ cup (125 mL) chopped cooked bacon
½ cup (125 mL) plain Greek yogurt
¼ cup (60 mL) mayonnaise
1 tsp (5 mL) Dijon mustard
1 garlic clove, shoot removed, chopped
1 tsp (5 mL) apple cider vinegar

Chicken thighs

2 tbsp (30 mL) smoked paprika
2 tbsp (30 mL) onion powder
1 tbsp (15 mL) garlic powder
1 tsp (5 mL) granulated sugar
1 tbsp (15 mL) salt
Cayenne pepper (optional)
12 boneless chicken thighs
1 tbsp (15 mL) vegetable oil

For serving (optional)

Zest and juice of 1 lemon
Fresh dill

1. Preheat the oven to 450°F (230°C). Line a baking sheet with parchment paper.

2. **Potato salad.** In a large saucepan filled with salted water, boil potatoes until tender. Drain and place on the prepared baking sheet. Flatten potatoes one by one with the bottom of a glass and spread them out so they don't touch. Oil them well and add salt and pepper to your taste.

3. Roast for 25 to 30 minutes or until potatoes are golden and crispy, turning them halfway through cooking. Let cool completely.

4. Meanwhile, in a large salad bowl, combine cucumber, green onions, dill, radishes, leeks, bacon, yogurt, mayo, Dijon mustard, garlic and apple cider vinegar. Add potatoes, salt and pepper to your taste, and mix well. Cover and refrigerate.

5. **Chicken thighs.** In a bowl, combine smoked paprika, onion powder, garlic powder, sugar, salt, and cayenne pepper to your taste, if desired. Season the thighs with the mixture to your taste.

6. In a large skillet, over high heat, heat oil and cook the thighs until browned on all sides and the internal temperature reaches 165°F (74°C). Let rest for 5 minutes.

7. Serve the chicken thighs with a big scoop of potato salad. If desired, garnish the potato salad with lemon zest, and the chicken with lemon juice and dill to your taste.

CHICKEN LEGS + ROASTED CARROTS + PISTACHIOS + FETA

Where the cut comes from: the leg

Serves
4 typical eaters or
2 atypical eaters
Prep time – 25 min
Cooking time – 1 hour 15 min

Parsley and feta salad

⅓ cup (75 mL) finely chopped fresh parsley

¼ cup (60 mL) crumbled feta cheese

1 tsp (5 mL) hot pepper flakes

Zest and juice of 1 lemon

¼ cup (60 mL) coarsely crushed pistachios

Roasted carrots

4 large carrots

¼ cup (60 mL) melted butter

3 tbsp (45 mL) balsamic vinegar

1 tsp (5 mL) honey + a drizzle (for serving)

Chicken legs

Salt

4 chicken leg quarters with skin and bones

Garlic yogurt

1 cup (250 mL) plain yogurt

1 to 2 garlic cloves, shoots removed, finely chopped

Salt and pepper

1. Preheat the oven to 375°F (190°C).

2. **Parsley and feta salad.** In a bowl, combine parsley, feta, hot pepper flakes, and lemon zest and juice. Refrigerate.

3. **Roasted carrots.** Peel carrots and cut in half lengthwise, then in half crosswise. In a baking dish, combine butter, balsamic vinegar and 1 tsp (5 mL) honey. Add carrots and mix well.

4. Cover with foil and bake for 15 minutes. Uncover and continue cooking for 25 to 30 minutes, or until the carrots are tender and nicely browned. Set aside; keep warm. (Leave the oven on.)

5. **Chicken legs.** Evenly salt the chicken legs to your taste. Arrange on a wire rack placed on a baking sheet or roasting pan. Bake for 30 minutes, or until the internal temperature reaches 165°F (74°C).

6. **Garlic yogurt.** In a bowl, combine yogurt and garlic; season with salt and pepper to your taste.

7. Stir pistachios into the parsley and feta salad. On the serving plates, spread a large spoonful of garlic yogurt and place roasted carrots on top. Add parsley and feta salad. Top with a drizzle of honey. Add one chicken leg and serve.

Note

This recipe can also be made on a barbecue grill. Cook the carrots over indirect heat in a covered oven-proof skillet. On high heat, over direct heat, sear the chicken legs until browned, then continue cooking over indirect heat until the internal temperature reaches 165°F (74°C).

ROAST CHICKEN +
AJI VERDE

If you have leftovers, they will be perfect for lunch the next day. Use them in tacos or in a club sandwich with the aji verde instead of mayo for a twist!

Serves
4 hungry folks or
2 really hungry folks
Prep time – 25 min
Cooking time – 1 hour

Roast chicken

2 tbsp (30 mL) chili powder

2 tbsp (30 mL) dried thyme

2 tbsp (30 mL) onion powder

2 tbsp (30 mL) garlic powder

3 tbsp (45 mL) smoked paprika

1 whole chicken, about 3 lbs (1.5 kg)

1 lemon, halved

Aji verde sauce

½ cup (125 mL) mayonnaise

½ cup (125 mL) sour cream

2 cups (500 mL) fresh cilantro leaves

Jalapeño to taste

1 to 2 garlic cloves, shoots removed

⅓ cup (75 mL) grated Parmesan

Zest and juice of 1 lime

¼ tsp (1 mL) salt

1. Preheat the oven to 350ºF (180ºC).

2. **Roast chicken.** In a bowl, combine chili powder, thyme, onion powder, garlic powder and smoked paprika. Season the chicken with the seasoning mixture to your taste. Insert lemon halves in the chicken cavity.

3. Place the chicken on a wire rack on a rimmed baking sheet or roasting pan. Bake for 1 hour, or until the internal temperature reaches 165ºF (74ºC).

4. **Aji verde sauce.** In a food processor or blender, blend all the ingredients. It's normal for this sauce not to be smooth.

5. To serve, cut the chicken into pieces and serve with the aji verde sauce.

CORNISH HENS + POTATOES + THYME + LEMON

Serves
4 ordinary eaters or
2 uncommon eaters
Prep time – 25 min
Cooking time – 1 hour

Baby potato skewers

4 large sprigs of rosemary

12 baby potatoes

1 lemon, sliced

2 onions, sliced

1 garlic bulb, about ¼ inch (0.5 cm) of top trimmed off

2 sprigs of thyme

1 tbsp (15 mL) herbes de Provence

½ cup (125 mL) dry white wine

2 tbsp (30 mL) fig jam

1 tbsp (15 mL) Dijon mustard

2 tbsp (30 mL) vegetable oil

Salt and pepper

Cornish hens

6 tbsp (90 mL) melted butter

1 tbsp (15 mL) fig jam

1 tsp (5 mL) dried thyme

2 Cornish hens

1 lemon, halved

Salt and pepper

1. Preheat the oven to 350°F (180°C).

2. **Baby potato skewers.** Partially remove the leaves from rosemary sprigs, keeping those at the ends (see photo). Set aside the other leaves for another use. With a skewer, pierce the center of each potato. Skewer 3 potatoes on each rosemary sprig.

3. In a baking dish, place sliced lemon and onion, garlic bulb (cut side down), sprigs of thyme and herbes de Provence. Add white wine, fig jam and Dijon mustard. Stir well.

4. Oil the skewered potatoes and place them on top of the mixture in the baking dish. Add salt and pepper to your taste. Set aside.

5. **Cornish hens.** In a bowl, combine melted butter, fig jam and thyme. Brush all over the hens and inside the cavities. Insert half a lemon in the cavity of each hen. Add salt and pepper to your taste. Arrange the hens on the potato skewers.

6. Bake for 45 minutes to 1 hour, or until the internal temperature reaches 165°F (74°C).

7. Squeeze the garlic bulb to remove the cloves and stir into the sauce before serving.

DUCK BREAST + ORANGE SODA + GINGER + CARROT PEARLS

⋮

I love serving this duck breast with mashed carrots. Orange is the new quack!

Serves
2 restrained people or
1 frantic person
Prep time – 25 min
Freezing time – 45 min
Tempering – 20 min
Cooking time – 30 min
Resting time – 5 to 10 min

Carrot pearls

2 cups (500 mL) vegetable oil

⅓ cup (75 mL) carrot juice

½ tsp (2 mL) agar-agar

Citrus salad

Segments of 1 peeled orange

Segments of 1 peeled pink
  grapefruit

5 fresh basil leaves, finely
  chopped

Zest and juice of 1 lemon

Salt and pepper

Duck breast

1 full boneless duck breast with
  skin

2 cans (each 12 oz/355 mL)
  orange soda

1 tbsp (15 mL) grated fresh
  gingerroot

Salt

Equipment

1 eye-dropper (available at
  pharmacies)

1. Carrot pearls. Pour oil into a tall container, like a juice glass, and put it in the freezer for 45 minutes before making the pearls.

2. Citrus salad. Cut orange and grapefruit segments in thirds and place in a bowl. Add basil and lemon zest and juice. Season with salt and pepper to your taste. Refrigerate.

3. In a small saucepan, over high heat, combine carrot juice and agar-agar; bring to a boil. Remove from the heat and fill the eye-dropper with the hot liquid.

4. Remove oil from the freezer. One drop at a time, add the carrot juice mixture into the oil; the pearls will solidify when they come into contact with the oil (see Note, page 68). Turn all the liquid into carrot pearls in this way.

5. Strain oil in a sieve to keep only the pearls. Immerse the pearls in a bowl of cold water to remove the excess oil. Strain again, place them in a bowl, cover, then store the pearls in the fridge.

6. Duck breast. Score the skin side of the breast with a sharp knife in a very fine cross-hatch pattern. Cut the breast into two halves. Let sit at room temperature on a wire rack for at least 20 minutes.

7. Pour orange soda into a saucepan and bring to a boil over high heat. Boil for 10 to 15 minutes, or until it has the consistency of syrup. Add fresh ginger and remove from the heat. Set aside.

8. Evenly salt the duck to your taste. In a skillet, over high heat, place the duck breasts skin side down and cook until brown on all sides. Pour in the orange syrup and ginger to coat the meat well. Remove from the heat and let rest for 5 to 10 minutes.

9. To serve, cut each piece of breast in half. Arrange on the plate, add the citrus salad between the slices and garnish with a few carrot pearls and drops of the syrup from the pan.

TURKEY DOM-PLINGS +
SWEET AND SOUR + CRANBERRIES

Makes
about 30 DOM-plings
Prep time – 45 min
Cooking time – 20 to 25 min

Cranberry sauce

¼ cup (60 mL) water

1 tbsp (15 mL) honey

½ cup (125 mL) granulated sugar

2 cups (500 mL) frozen cranberries

A piece of fresh gingerroot

DOM-plings

Cooking oil

8 oz (250 g) ground turkey

2 green onions, finely chopped

2 tbsp (30 mL) finely chopped fresh
gingerroot

1 garlic clove, shoot removed, finely
chopped

2 tsp (10 mL) toasted sesame oil

1 tbsp (15 mL) soy sauce

Sambal oelek or sriracha sauce to taste

1 pkg (1 lb/454 g) store-bought wonton
wrappers

Salt

1. **Cranberry sauce.** In a saucepan, over high heat, bring to a boil water, honey and sugar. Add cranberries and ginger, and stir. Bring to a boil again and simmer for 5 to 10 minutes over medium heat. Remove from the heat.

2. Remove the piece of ginger. In a food processor or blender, blend the mixture until it forms a smooth purée. Set aside.

3. **DOM-plings.** In a large saucepan or deep fryer, heat enough oil to immerse the DOM-plings for deep-frying to 350°F (180°C). In a bowl, combine ground turkey, green onions, ginger, garlic, sesame oil, soy sauce and sambal oelek or sriracha sauce.

4. On a clean worktop, spread out wonton wrappers. Stuff each wrapper with 1 tsp (5 mL) of turkey mixture. Fold and seal the seam with a little water.

5. Fry the DOM-plings, in batches as necessary, for 10 to 15 minutes, turning if necessary, until golden and cooked inside.

6. Place the DOM-plings on a wire rack and salt lightly to your taste.

7. Reheat the cranberry sauce, if needed, and serve with the fried DOM-plings.

Notes

In step 5, you can also boil the dumplings in water for 3 minutes, drain and then fry them in the skillet in a little vegetable oil.

Another option to try for dipping: garlic and toasted sesame mayo! In a bowl, combine 1 cup (250 mL) mayonnaise, 1 garlic clove, shoot removed, finely chopped, and 2 tsp (10 mL) toasted sesame oil. It might sound strange, but the creamy texture is delicious with the sweet and sour notes of the cranberries!

QUAILS + SPATCHCOCKED + PEANUT SAUCE + GRILLED BOK CHOY

Serves
2 regular eaters or
1 aggressive eater
Prep time – 15 min
Cooking time – 30 min

Peanut sauce

½ cup (125 mL) chicken stock or water

3 tbsp (45 mL) rice vinegar

3 tbsp (45 mL) soy sauce

6 tbsp (90 mL) smooth peanut butter

1 tbsp (15 mL) granulated sugar

2 tbsp (30 mL) toasted sesame oil

1½ tsp (7 mL) sambal oelek or sriracha sauce (optional)

1 tbsp (15 mL) grated fresh gingerroot

1 garlic clove, shoot removed, finely chopped

Spatchcocked quails

Salt

2 spatchcocked quails

Bok choy

4 small bok choy, cut in half lengthwise

2 tbsp (30 mL) vegetable oil

Salt and pepper

12 oz (375 g) wide rice noodles

For serving (optional)

Green onion, thinly sliced on the diagonal

Sesame seeds

1. **Peanut sauce.** In a bowl, stir together all the ingredients. Set aside.

2. Preheat the barbecue to high on just one side of the grill; for a charcoal grill, use a charcoal chimney starter to get glowing coals and place it at one end of the grill.

3. **Spatchcocked quails.** Evenly salt the quails to your taste. Place the grill over direct heat or in the coals. Sear the quails until nicely browned on all sides, turning halfway through cooking. If pieces of charcoal stick to the meat, remove them with tongs. Move the quails over indirect heat and continue cooking for about 15 minutes, or until the internal temperature reaches 165°F (74°C).

4. **Bok choy.** Toss the bok choy in oil, then add salt and pepper. Place on the grill over direct heat. Cook until nicely browned, turning halfway through cooking.

5. Cook the rice noodles according to the package instructions. Drain.

6. In a saucepan, over medium heat, heat the peanut sauce.

7. To serve, place the rice noodles on the plates and drizzle with peanut sauce to your taste. Arrange one quail and two grilled bok choy on top. If desired, garnish with green onion and sesame seeds.

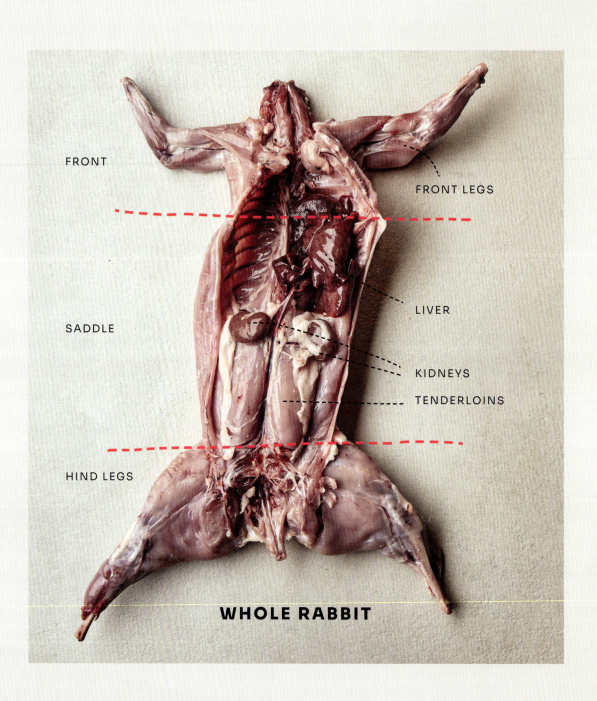

FRONT

FRONT LEGS

LIVER

SADDLE

KIDNEYS

TENDERLOINS

HIND LEGS

WHOLE RABBIT

farmed game

You may be surprised to learn that game that is available at the butcher is farmed, not hunted. Wild game must be butchered and sold in specialty butcher shops to guarantee that the meat is safe to eat and to avoid possible contamination with other types of meat. Broadly speaking, before selling meat at a butcher shop, the butcher must make sure it complies with certain standards and has been inspected by professionals. Given that the history of a wild animal cannot be determined (date of birth, diet, diseases and so on), it is handled in a certain way.

Farmed game brings together two main families: large game (deer, boar, bison, wapiti, ostrich, etc.) and small game (hare, rabbit, goose, partridge, quail, pheasant, guinea fowl, pigeon, etc.). You will have noticed that some poultry appears on these lists. They are part of the subcategory of feathered game, also called game birds . . . and often they are simply classified as poultry!

In the small game category are found several lagomorph mammals of the Leporidae family, such as hare and rabbit. Fun (and at times confusing) fact: In the fields of butchering and cooking, they fall under the category of . . . poultry. For rabbits, the word "breast" is not used: the saddle is the loin and the rib. Rabbits don't have wings, so they are simply called front legs.

Game meat is consumed much less than the meat of other livestock. Because it is so much less common, game is more expensive than other meats, but people enjoy it for its sophisticated flavors. GAME on!

RABBIT + SPATCHCOCKED + VIETNAMESE STYLE

Serves
4 calm eaters or
2 excited eaters
Prep time – 25 min
Cooking time – 1 hour 40 min

Vietnamese seasoning

Zest of 1 lime

Juice of 2 limes

4 green onions, finely chopped

¼ cup (60 mL) packed brown sugar

2 garlic cloves, shoots removed, finely chopped

3 tbsp (45 mL) vegetable oil

⅓ cup (75 mL) fresh cilantro or mint, finely chopped

3 tbsp (45 mL) fish sauce

1 tbsp (15 mL) grated fresh gingerroot

1 tsp (5 mL) sriracha sauce or sambal oelek (optional)

Salt

Rabbit

2 tbsp (30 mL) butter

1 tbsp (15 mL) vegetable oil

1 whole spatchcocked rabbit

2 cans (14 oz/400 mL each) coconut milk

For serving (optional)

Green onions, finely chopped on the diagonal

1 bird's eye chile pepper, thinly sliced on the diagonal

Fresh cilantro, finely chopped

Lime zest and juice

1. Vietnamese seasoning. In a bowl, combine all the ingredients. Set aside.

2. Rabbit. In a Dutch oven or large saucepan, over high heat, melt butter and oil. Sear the rabbit on all sides until nicely browned. Add the Vietnamese seasoning and coconut milk, and stir.

3. Cover and simmer over low heat for 1 hour and 30 minutes, or until the meat comes off the bone easily.

4. Serve whole on a wooden board and, if desired, garnish with green onions, bird's eye chile pepper, cilantro, and lime zest and juice.

Note

This recipe works well on the barbecue. Simply grill the rabbit over direct heat, then transfer it to a Dutch oven. Add Vietnamese seasoning and coconut milk. Continue cooking, covered, on low over indirect heat.

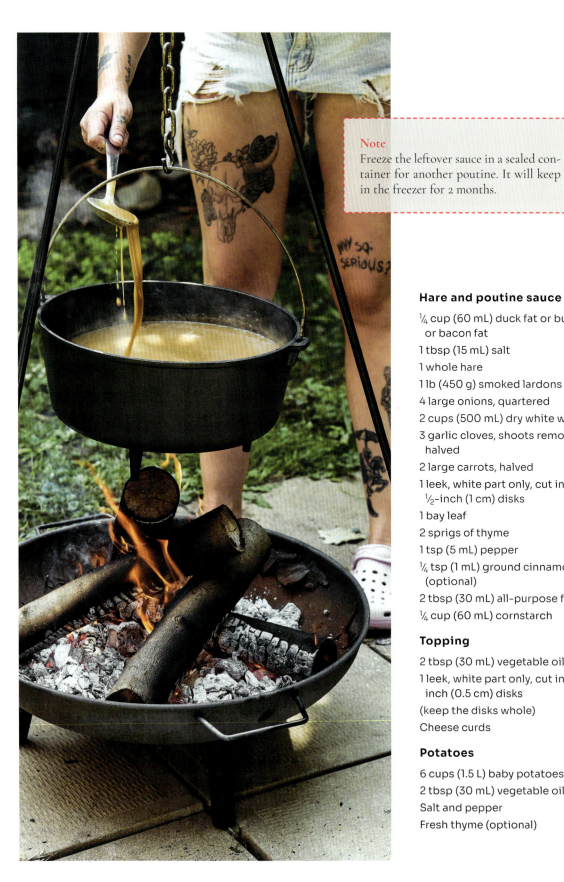

Note

Freeze the leftover sauce in a sealed container for another poutine. It will keep in the freezer for 2 months.

Hare and poutine sauce

¼ cup (60 mL) duck fat or butter or bacon fat

1 tbsp (15 mL) salt

1 whole hare

1 lb (450 g) smoked lardons

4 large onions, quartered

2 cups (500 mL) dry white wine

3 garlic cloves, shoots removed, halved

2 large carrots, halved

1 leek, white part only, cut into ½-inch (1 cm) disks

1 bay leaf

2 sprigs of thyme

1 tsp (5 mL) pepper

¼ tsp (1 mL) ground cinnamon (optional)

2 tbsp (30 mL) all-purpose flour

¼ cup (60 mL) cornstarch

Topping

2 tbsp (30 mL) vegetable oil

1 leek, white part only, cut into ¼-inch (0.5 cm) disks

(keep the disks whole)

Cheese curds

Potatoes

6 cups (1.5 L) baby potatoes, halved

2 tbsp (30 mL) vegetable oil

Salt and pepper

Fresh thyme (optional)

HARE + POUTINE + LEEKS

I love this hare poutine with baby potatoes. Seared leeks add a touch of something special and work beautifully with the other ingredients in this gourmet version of poutine!

Serves – 4 distinguished people or 2 people whose neurons are misfiring
Prep time – 45 min   **Cooking time** – 4 hours

1. Hare and poutine sauce. In a large saucepan, over high heat, melt duck fat. Evenly salt the hare. Sear on all sides until nicely browned. Remove the hare from the saucepan and set aside on a plate.

2. In the same saucepan, sauté lardons. When they start to brown, set aside on a plate.

3. Put the hare back in the saucepan and add onions. When onions are golden, deglaze with white wine, scraping the bottom with a wooden spoon to get all the brown bits. Boil until the liquid is reduced by half.

4. Add garlic, carrots, leek, bay leaf, thyme, pepper and, if desired, cinnamon. Cover with cold water and bring to a boil. Simmer over low heat, uncovered, for 2 to 3 hours, or until the meat comes off the bones easily. Set aside the hare on a plate and let cool.

5. Strain the cooking liquid and vegetables through a sieve into a bowl (discard solids). Return the strained sauce to the saucepan, add lardons and bring to a boil.

6. In a bowl, combine flour and cornstarch, then gradually add cold water until you get a consistency of thick glue. With a whisk, gradually add just enough to the sauce mixture to thicken it to the desired consistency (you may not need to add the whole mixture). Boil until the raw flour taste is cooked out. Remove from the heat.

7. Remove bones from the hare with your fingers (be careful not to leave any small bones in) and set the meat aside.

8. Topping. In a skillet, over high heat, heat oil and add leeks. When they start to char, turn them over, then turn off the heat. Set aside.

9. Preheat the oven to 425°F (220°C). Line one or two rimmed baking sheets with parchment paper.

10. Potatoes. In a large bowl, mix the potatoes, oil, salt, pepper and, if desired, thyme to your taste. Place the potatoes, cut side down, on the prepared baking sheet(s).

11. Bake for 20 to 30 minutes, or until the potatoes are golden on the outside and soft on the inside.

12. To serve, place the potatoes in a shallow dish. Add in this order: half the cheese curds, hare pieces, lots of sauce, cheese curds (again) and seared leeks.

VENISON RIB CHOPS + SEA BUCKTHORN + BACON MARMALADE

Serves
2 disciplined people or
1 undisciplined person
Prep time – 45 min
Tempering – 15 min
Cooking time – 1 hour 20 min
Resting time – 5 min

Venison ribs

2 Frenched venison rib chops (or
  venison medallions), 2 inches (5 cm)
  thick
Salt
3 tbsp (45 mL) vegetable oil

Bacon and sea buckthorn berry marmalade

12 oz (375 g) bacon, cut into matchsticks
4 white onions, diced
¼ cup (60 mL) butter
¾ cup (175 mL) pure maple syrup
½ cup (125 mL) whiskey (or beer or wine
  or other alcohol of your choice)
¼ cup (60 mL) white wine vinegar
¼ cup (60 mL) frozen sea buckthorn
  berries

Garnish

Finely chopped fresh chives

1. Venison ribs. Unwrap the chops and let sit at room temperature on a wire rack for 15 minutes.

2. Bacon and sea buckthorn berry marmalade. In a saucepan, over medium-high heat, sauté bacon until browned. Add onions, butter, maple syrup, whiskey and white wine vinegar. Simmer over low heat for about 1 hour, or until the texture is thick and sticky. Remove from the heat, add sea buckthorn berries, stir and set aside.

3. Preheat the oven to 350°F (180°C).

4. Evenly salt the meat to your taste. In an oven-proof skillet, over medium-high heat, heat oil and sear the chops until nicely browned, turning them halfway through cooking.

5. Transfer the skillet to the oven and bake for 5 to 10 minutes, or until the internal temperature reaches 127°F (53°C) for very rare or to desired doneness. Let rest on a wire rack 5 minutes.

6. To serve, pour hot marmalade evenly over the ribs and sprinkle with chives. Delicious with mashed potatoes and root vegetables!

Note

This recipe also works well on the barbecue. Over high heat, sear chops over direct heat until nicely browned, then continue cooking over indirect heat until the temperature reaches 127°F (53°C) or to desired doneness. The marmalade can also be made over indirect heat.

WILD BOAR RIBS + HASKAP BERRIES + GARLIC CHIPS

Serves – 2 disciplined people or 1 rebellious person
Preparation – 45 min   **Tempering** – 15 min   **Cooking time** – 3 hours

Boar ribs

1 rack of wild boar ribs, about 3⅓ lbs (1.5 kg)

Salt and pepper

8 garlic cloves, shoots removed, halved

7 tbsp (105 mL) vegetable oil, divided

2 shallots, finely chopped

¼ cup (60 mL) butter

½ cup (125 mL) balsamic vinegar

2 tbsp (30 mL) honey

1 sprig of fresh thyme

⅓ cup (75 mL) haskap berries (honeyberries), frozen or fresh

Fried garlic chips

Cooking oil

3 garlic cloves, shoots removed, sliced with a mandolin

Salt

1. Boar ribs. Unwrap the ribs and let sit at room temperature on a wire rack for at least 15 minutes.

2. Fried garlic chips. In a saucepan or deep fryer, heat enough oil to immerse garlic for deep frying to 350°F (180°C). Fry garlic slices until golden. Place them, one at a time, on a paper towel and salt well. Set aside.

3. Preheat the oven to 350°F (180°C).

4. Salt and pepper the ribs to your taste. Place garlic cloves in the middle of a large sheet of foil. Add 5 tbsp (75 mL) of oil and stir. Arrange the ribs on top (meat side down and bone side up). Fold the foil to make a pouch. Wrap in a second layer of foil to seal it as tightly as possible.

5. Bake for about 2 hours and 30 minutes, or until the meat is coming off the bone.

6. In a large skillet, over high heat, heat the remaining 2 tbsp (30 mL) oil and sauté shallots for 3 minutes. Add butter and let foam until golden brown. Deglaze with balsamic vinegar, scraping the bottom with a wooden spoon to get all the browned bits. Add honey and thyme and boil until liquid is reduced by half or until it has a syrupy texture.

7. Remove the sauce from heat. Add haskap berries and stir. Slice the ribs and add them to the heated sauce, coating them well.

8. Serve with garlic chips and roasted vegetables, such as parsnips and Nantes carrots.

ROASTED PARTRIDGE +
PAN-FRIED RADISHES + GARLIC YOGURT

Serves – 2 disciplined people or 1 unpredictable person
Prep time – 45 min   **Cooking time** – 1 hour 40 min

Partridge

2 tbsp (30 mL) soft butter
2 tbsp (30 mL) Dijon mustard
2 partridges
Salt and pepper
2 leeks, white part only, halved
  lengthwise
2 carrots, halved lengthwise
2 onions, quartered
2 sprigs of fresh thyme
3 garlic cloves, shoots removed, crushed
2 cups (500 mL) poultry stock
1 cup (250 mL) dry white wine

Garlic yogurt sauce

2 cups (500 mL) plain yogurt
Zest of 1 lemon
Juice of ½ lemon
4 garlic cloves, shoots removed, finely
  chopped

Pan-fried radishes

2 tbsp (30 mL) vegetable oil
12 radishes, cut in half lengthwise
3 shallots, cut in half lengthwise
¼ cup (60 mL) butter
2 or 3 sprigs of thyme
4 garlic cloves, shoots removed,
  crushed
Salt and pepper

For serving

Lemon zest
Fresh parsley leaves (optional)
Thin cucumber ribbons (optional)

1. Preheat the oven to 350°F (180°C).
2. **Partridge.** In a bowl, combine butter and Dijon mustard until smooth. Baste the partridges with the mixture. Sprinkle with salt and pepper to your taste. Set aside.
3. Place leeks, carrots, onions, thyme and garlic in a roasting pan. Arrange the partridges on top of the vegetables. Pour poultry stock and white wine into the pan.
4. Cover with foil and bake for 45 minutes. Increase the oven temperature to 425°F (220°C), uncover and continue cooking for about 30 minutes. The partridges are done when they are nicely browned and the internal temperature reaches 165°F (74°C).
5. **Garlic yogurt sauce.** In a bowl, combine all the ingredients. Cover and refrigerate.
6. **Pan-fried radishes.** In a skillet, over high heat, heat oil and cook the radishes and shallots. When they are starting to brown, add butter, thyme and garlic. Let butter foam (without burning) and baste the vegetables with a spoon. Add salt and pepper. Set aside.
7. On a serving plate, place two large spoonfuls of garlic yogurt sauce, then spread out the grilled radishes and shallots on top. Add the partridge. Pour a little hot butter on the vegetables. Garnish with the lemon zest, parsley and a few cucumber ribbons, if desired.

APPENDICES

MEAT TRANSLATOR

NAMES OF **BEEF** CUTS			
English	**Alternate English**	**Quebec French**	**French**
CROSS RIB			
Shoulder		Épaule	Raquette
Shoulder cross rib roast	Cross rib pot roast, chuck arm roast, clod roast, book roast, Boston cut, bread and butter cut, English cut roast, shoulder center roast	Rôti de côtes croisées	
Chuck short ribs	Braising short ribs, simmering short ribs, English short ribs, middle ribs	Côtes à braiser	Travers de bœuf
Shoulder clod	Chuck shoulder clod	Pointe d'épaule	
Shoulder clod steak	Arm chuck steak, ranch steak	Bifteck de pointe d'épaule	
Shoulder clod roast	Arm roast, clod roast, shoulder center roast, shoulder roast	Rôti de pointe d'épaule	
Shoulder petite tender	*Teres major*, shoulder clod petite tender, petite tender	Filet d'épaule	Filet d'épaule
SHANK (FORE AND HIND)			
Frenched shank	Thor's hammer, hammer shank	Jarret à manchon	Jarret manchonné
Hindshank	Back shank	Jarret arrière	Gîte arrière
Foreshank	Front shank	Jarret avant	Gîte avant
Center cut shank		Jarret centre	Gîte coupe du centre
Sliced shank	Osso buco, osso buco-style centre-cut shank	Tranche de jarret	Gîte tranché
Bone marrow		Os à moelle	Os à moelle
Banana shank	Red tail	La carotte (gousse d'ail)	Nerveux de gîte à la noix

NAMES OF **BEEF** CUTS

BRISKET/PLATE

English	Alternate English	Quebec French	French
Whole brisket	Full brisket	Pointe de poitrine + poitrine	Caparaçon
Brisket flat half	Brisket flat end, brisket flat cut, brisket middle cut, brisket front cut, brisket first cut	Poitrine (plat)	
Brisket point half	Brisket point end, brisket double, brisket deckle, brisket point cut, brisket nose cut, brisket second cut	Pointe de poitrine	Caparaçon gros bout
Plate short ribs	Short ribs, flanken style ribs, dino ribs	Bouts de côtes	Plat de côtes
Korean short ribs	Flanken style short ribs, cross-cut short ribs, sliced short ribs, kalbi, galbi, Miami style short ribs, Maui style short ribs	Bouts de côtes tranchés à la coréenne	
Frenched short ribs		Carré de bouts de côtes	Plat de côtes manchonné
Asado-cut short ribs		Tranche de bouts de côtes (2.5 cm/1 in et +)	Tranche de plat de côtes complet (4 côtes)
Skirt steak		Hampe	Hampe/manteau

RIB

English	Alternate English	Quebec French	French
Prime rib roast	Rib roast, rib roast (bone-in), standing rib roast, côtes de bœuf roast, export rib	Rôti de côtes	Rôti de côtes
Ribeye roast (boneless)	Entrecôte roast, boneless prime rib roast, boneless rib roast	Rôti de faux-filet	Rôti de contre-filet
Rib steak (bone in)	Prime rib steak, Frenched rib steak, cowboy steak	Bifteck de côtes	Côte de bœuf
Complexus		Complexus	Complexus
Longissimus dorsi		Longissimus dorsi	Longissimus dorsi
Ribeye steak (boneless)	Entrecôte	Bifteck de faux-filet	Contre-filet
Ribeye cap	*Spinalis* (Latin)	Spinalis	Spinalis
Hanger steak	Hanging tender	Onglet	Onglet
Back ribs	Rack of ribs, rib bones, finger ribs	Côtes levées de bœuf	

BLADE

English	Alternate English	Quebec French	French
Blade chuck roast	Blade pot roast, 7-bone chuck roast, 7-bone pot roast, bone-in chuck arm pot roast, bone-in chuck	Rôti de palette (bas de palette + œil + macreuse)	Basses côtes + jumeau + paleron avec os
Flat iron steak	Top blade steak, shoulder top blade steak, top blade filet, book steak, butler steak	Bifteck de macreuse	Paleron à griller

English	Alternate English	Quebec French	French
Flat iron	Top blade	Macreuse	Paleron
Chuck eye steak	Delmonico steak, boneless chuck filet steak, English steak	Bifteck faux-filet (palette)	Tranche de basse côte
Chuck tender	Chuck filet, chuck eye, medallion pot roast, mock tender, Scotch tender	Œil palette	Jumeaux
Chuck roll roast	Bottom blade roast	Rôti de bas de palette	Basse côte + divers autres muscles
Denver steak	Chuck flap, chuck flap tail, chuck under blade center steak, chuck under blade steak	Bifteck Denver	Le persillé
Top blade		Haut de palette	Paleron + jumeau
Surprise steak		La surprise (muscle dans le bas de palette)	Surprise de bœuf
HEAD			
Cheek		Joues	Joues
Tongue		Langue	Langue
ROUND			
Top round	Inside round	Intérieur de ronde	Tendre de tranche
Top round roast	Inside round roast	Rôti intérieur de ronde	Rôti de tendre de tranche
Top round steak	Inside round steak, London broil, top round steak cap off/on	Bifteck de ronde	Tendre de tranche
Adductor	Inside tender, tender top muscle	Grosse poire	Grosse poire
Bullet muscle	*Gracillis*	Petite poire	Poire
Pectineus		Le merlan de ronde	Le merlan
Outside round steak	Bottom round steak, Western steak, outside round flat, outside round heel	Bifteck d'extérieur de ronde	
Tenderized round steak	French steak	Bifteck français	
Eye of round (roast or steak)	Round eye pot roast	Œil de ronde	Rond de gîte
LOIN			
T-bone steak	Porterhouse (large filet portion)	Bifteck d'aloyau	
Bone-in strip loin roast		Coquille d'aloyau	Faux-filet sur os
Strip steak	Strip loin steak, top loin steak, New York strip steak, New York steak	Bifteck de contre-filet	Faux-filet

NAMES OF **BEEF** CUTS

English	Alternate English	Quebec French	French
Bone-in strip steak	Bone-in strip loin steak, bone-in wing steak, bone-in New York strip steak, bone-in top loin steak, ambassador steak, club steak, hotel style steak, Kansas City strip steak, shell steak	Bifteck de contre-filet sur os	Faux-filet sur os
Strip roast	Top loin roast, strip loin roast, New York roast	Rôti de contre-filet	Rôti de faux-filet
Whole tenderloin	Whole filet	Filet mignon (complet)	Filet complet
Tenderloin roast	Filet roast, Châteaubriand roast	Rôti de filet	Filet en rôti
Tenderloin steak	Filet steak, filet mignon, tenderloin medallion	Bifteck de filet mignon	Médaillon de filet de bœuf, châteaubriand (bardé ou non)
Center cut tenderloin	Center-cut filet	Filet centre	Cœur du filet
Tenderloin tail		Queue de filet	Pointe de filet
Tenderloin chain		Chaînette filet mignon	Chaînette du filet
Wing steak		Bifteck de côtes d'aloyau	
Wing rib roast		Rôti de côtes d'aloyau, T-bone partie sans filet	Faux-filet sur os
SIRLOIN			
Sirloin		Surlonge	Rumsteak
Sirloin steak (whole)		Bifteck de surlonge	Bifteck rumsteak + aiguillette rumsteak
Fausse araignée (false spider)		Fausse araignée	Fausse araignée
Mouse steak		Langue de chat	Langue de chat
Oyster steak (in the groin)	Spider steak	L'araignée de boeuf (dans l'aine)	
Bottom sirloin tri-tip (roast or steak)	Bottom sirloin, Newport (roast or steak), Santa Maria (roast or steak), tri tip (roast or steak), triangle (roast or steak)	Triangle de bas de surlonge	Aiguillette baronne
Top sirloin steak (boneless)		Bifteck de surlonge désossé	Bifteck rumsteak + aiguillette désossée
Top sirloin roast (boneless)	Top sirloin butt roast	Rôti de surlonge désossé	Rôti de rumsteak + aiguillette rumsteak
Top sirloin butt steak (center-cut)	Top sirloin heart, top sirloin cap off/removed, baseball steak, Boston steak	Cœur de surlonge	Filet de rumsteak
Top sirloin steak		Bifteck de haut de surlonge	Bifteck cœur de rumsteak
Top sirloin butt steak, tenderloin off		Bifteck de surlonge sans filet	Rumsteak + aiguillette Rumsteak sans filet
Sirloin bavette steak	Bottom sirloin flap steak, bottom sirloin bavette steak, bottom sirloin butt (flap), flap steak, flap meat	Bifteck de bavette	Bavette d'aloyau

NAMES OF **BEEF** CUTS

English	Alternate English	Quebec French	French
Tenderloin head	Tenderloin butt, butt tender, arrow head	Tête de filet complete	Tête de filet
Coulotte (roast or steak)	Picanha (Brazil), top sirloin cap (roast or steak), sirloin cap (roast or steak), rump cap	Culotte	Aiguillette rumsteak
FLANK			
Flank steak		Bifteck de flanc	Bavette de flanchet
Whole flank (primal cut)		Flanc nature	Flanchet + tendron + milieu poitrine
SIRLOIN TIP			
Sirloin tip eye roast	Sirloin tip side roast, knuckle side roast	Rôti pointe de surlonge (plat)	
Sirloin tip round roast	Sirloin tip center roast, round tip roast cap-off, sirloin tip roast, knuckle center roast	Rôti pointe de surlonge (rond)	
Sirloin tip steak		Bifteck de pointe de surlonge	Rond de tranche
Sandwich steak		Bifteck sandwich	Bœuf pour pierrade (équivalent)
RUMP			
Rump		Croupe	
Outside rump roast	Bottom round rump roast, bottom round roast	Rôti extérieur de croupe	
Inside rump roast		Rôti intérieur de croupe	
Boneless rump roast		Rôti de croupe désossé	
MISCELLANEOUS			
Kabob cubes	Cubes for skewers	Cubes à brochettes	Cubes à brochettes
Stew cubes	Cubes for stew, stewing cubes	Cubes à ragout	Cubes à mijoter
Lean stew cubes	Lean cubes for stew, lean stewing cubes	Cubes bourguignons	Cubes maigres à mijoter
Scaloppini	Escalopes	Escalope	Escalope
Fondue (thin slices)	Beef for hot pot (Chinese fondue)	Fondue chinoise	Fondue chinoise, pirade (similaire)
Strips	Stir-fry strips	Lanières	Émincé
Tenderized steak	Cubed steak, cube steak, minute steak, chicken fried steak, Swiss steak		Bifteck attendri

NAMES OF **PORK** CUTS

English	Alternate English	Quebec French	French
LOIN			
Loin		Longe	Carré de côtes + filet
Sirloin	Buckeye, chump	Surlonge	Quasi
Tenderloin		Filet de porc	Filet mignon, filet, mignon de porc
Center-cut loin roast	Loin center roast	Rôti de longe	Rôti de côte première ou seconde
Rib roast		Rôti de bouts de côtes	
Secretos (Spanish)		Grillade secrète de porc	Carbonade, grillade
Frenched rib roast	Frenched rack of pork, Frenched centre-cut rib roast, Frenched loin rib half	Carré de porc (côtes nettoyées à blanc)	Carré de porc manchonné
Crown roast	Rib crown roast, crown rib roast, crown roast of pork	Couronne de porc	Couronne de porc
Sirloin roast	Sirloin-end roast, loin end roast, hipbone roast, buckeye roast	Rôti bout de surlonge	
Sirloin chop	Buckeye chop, sirloin steak	Côtelette bout de surlonge	Côtelette de pointe
Boneless loin center chop	New York chop, America's cut (when 1-1/4-inch thick)	Côtelette centre désossée	Côte première ou seconde désossée
Bone-in center-cut chops (with tenderloin)	T-bone, porterhouse	Côtelette filet	Côte filet, côtelette de longe
Frenched center-cut chop	Frenched loin centre chop	Côtelette manchon (Côte bistro, côte française)	Côte de porc manchonée
Butterflied chop	Pork loin centre chop, butterflied	Côtelette papillon	Côtelette papillon
Loin rib chop	Rib chop, center-cut rib chop, chop end cut, rib cut chop, rib end cut	Côte de porc (sans filet)	Côte de porc
Back ribs	Baby back ribs, loin back ribs, loin ribs	Côtes levées de dos	Côtes levées de dos
SHOULDER			
Shoulder		Épaule	Échine + épaule
Butt	Blade, shoulder blade, Boston butt, Boston shoulder, shoulder	Bas de palette	Une partie de l'échine
Flat iron		Macreuse	paleron
Shoulder butt steak (bone-in or boneless)	Shoulder blade steak (bone-in or boneless), blade steak, shoulder steak, blade chop	Tranche de palette (avec ou sans os), (Le bikini)	Palette + paleron + jumeaux
Shoulder blade capicola	Shoulder butt capicola, collar butt, shoulder loin	Capicollo (une partie du soc capicole)	Capicollo (une partie de l'échine)
Money muscle	Coppa, collar	File d'épaule	Merlan d'épaule
La pluma (Spanish)		La plume	La plume
La presa (Spanish)		La presse	La presse

NAMES OF **PORK** CUTS			
English	**Alternate English**	**Quebec French**	**French**
Picnic shoulder roast	Picnic roast, shoulder arm picnic	Rôti de porc picnic	
Pork shoulder chop (rib section)		Côtelette découverte	Côte d'échine
Foreshank	Shoulder hock	Jarret (avant)	Jarret avant, noix de hachage
Foot		Pied	Pied
SIDE/BELLY			
Spareribs	Side ribs, St. Louis style ribs, St. Louis style spareribs, breastbone-off spareribs	Côtes levées de flanc	Travers
Bavette	Flap, flap steak	Bavette de porc	Bavette d'aloyau
Pork belly (sliced or whole)	Side (sliced or whole), lard	Flanc complet (avec or sans couenne)	Poitrine
Flank steak		Steak de flanc	Bavette de flanchet
Skirt		Hampe	Hampe
LEG			
Whole fresh ham roast	Whole leg roast	Rôti de fesse de porc complet	Jambon de porc
Shank end fresh ham roast	Leg shank portion roast, shank end leg roast	Rôti de fesse de porc bout du jarret	
Sirloin tip fresh ham roast	Sirloin tip leg roast	Rôti de pointe de surlonge	Rôti noix pâtissière
Sirloin half fresh ham roast	Sirloin half leg roast, sirloin half	Rôti de fesse, bout de croupe	
Inside fresh ham roast	Inside leg roast	Rôti de fesse de porc, intérieur	Rôti de noix de ronde
Outside fresh ham roast	Outside leg roast	Rôti de fesse de porc, extérieur	Rôti de sous noix de ronde
Fresh ham slice, mechanically tenderized	Leg slice, mechanically tenderized	Tranche de fesse attendrie	
Fresh ham steak	Leg steak, whole leg slice	Tranche de fesse de porc complète	Rouelle
Leg inside scaloppini	Inside round scaloppini, leg cutlet, escalope	Escalope de porc (intérieur)	Escalope de jambon
Spider muscle	Spider steak	Araignée	Araignée
Hindshank	Shank, hock, knuckle	Jarret (arrière)	Jarret jambon
HEAD AND TAIL			
Head	Whole head, half head	Tête de porc (complète ou demie)	Tête
Cheek		Joue de porc	Joue
Jowl		Bajoue	Gorge
Snout		Museau de porc	Grouin

NAMES OF **PORK** CUTS

English	Alternate English	Quebec French	French
Tongue		Langue de porc	Langue
Ear		Oreille de porc	Oreille
Neck		Collier	Collier
Tail		Queue de porc	Queue
MISCELLANEOUS			
Kabob cubes	Cubes for skewers, cubes for kabobs	Cubes de porc à brochettes	Cubes pour brochettes
Stewing cubes	Cubes for stew, stew cubes	Cubes de porc à ragoût	Cubes à mijoter
Paupiette	Stuffed bundles	Paupiette de porc	Paupiette
Strips		Lanières de porc	Émincés

NAMES OF **LAMB** CUTS

English	Alternate English	Quebec French	French
FRONT			
Whole boneless neck		Collier désossé complet	Collier d'agneau désossé
Sliced neck		Tranche de collier (os)	Tranche de collier
Whole shoulder		Épaule complète	Épaule
Shoulder with shank		Raquette (épaule + jarret)	Épaule levée + jarret
Boneless shoulder roast		Rôti d'épaule d'agneau	Épaule désossée et ficelée
Shoulder blade	Square cut shoulder	Rôti de palette	Épaule + côte découverte
Sliced square cut shoulder		Tranche de palette	Tranche de palette (épaule + côte découverte)
First ribs		Côtelette découverte	Côte découverte, Côte d'échine
Shoulder-end rib chops		1 res côtes (des côtes découvertes)	Côte royale
Shoulder arm chop		Tranche d'épaule avec os	Épaule tranchée
Breast		Poitrine	Épigramme
Rolled breast		Poitrine roulée	Épigramme roulé
Shank	Front shank, foreshank	Jarret (avant)	Jarret, jarret avant
LEG			
Frenched long leg		Gigot manchon	Gigot manchonné
Shank-end leg roast	Leg roast shank portion, leg roast chump off shank on	Rôti de bas de gigot	Gigot raccourci
Boneless leg roast		Rôti gigot désossé	Rôti de gigot désossé

NAMES OF **LAMB** CUTS

English	Alternate English	Quebec French	French
Butt-portion leg roast		Rôti de haut de gigot	Gigot raccourci
Sirloin roast		Rôti de surlonge	Selle
Center cut leg steak	Centre slice leg steak	Tranche de gigot (Steak de gigot)	Tranche de gigot
Hindshank	Back shank	Souris agneau (jarret arrière, jarret de gigot)	Souris
Boneless hindshank	Boneless back shank	Souris désossée	
RIB			
Rib roast	Rack of lamb	Carré d'agneau (os non à blanc)	Carré d'agneau
Frenched rib roast	Frenched rack	Carré d'agneau à manchon (os à blanc)	Carré d'agneau manchonné
Crown roast	Rib crown	Couronne d'agneau	Couronne
Rib chop		Côtelette bout de côte	Côte (première, seconde or royale)
Frenched rib chop		Côtelette manchon	Côte manchonée
Boneless ribeye		Faux-filet (désossé)	La noisette (partie du centre seulement)
Center cut rib chops		4 côtes (côté filet)	côtes secondes
Tenderloin-end rib chops		4 premières côtes (côté découvert)	Côtes premières
FLANK			
Spareribs	Flank sideribs, Denver ribs	Côtes levées de flanc	Travers
Whole flank (primal cut)	Whole belly	Flanc complet (Poitrine)	Poitrine + haut de côtelette
Stuffed boneless rolled flank	Stuffed belly	Flanc farci	Poitrine + haut de côtelette farci
Boneless rolled flank	Boneless rolled belly	Flanc roulé (farci ou non)	Pointrine + haut de côtelette roulé
LOIN			
Boneless loin roast		Contre-filet complet désossé	Noisette, canon 1er choix
Loin chop	T-bone	Côtelette filet	Côte filet
Tenderloin		Filet	File d'agneau, filet mignon

NAMES OF **VEAL** CUTS

English	Alternate English	Quebec French	French
BREAST (BRISKET)			
Whole breast	Full breast, full brisket	Pointe de poitrine + poitrine	Caparaçon

NAMES OF **VEAL** CUTS

English	Alternate English	Quebec French	French
CROSS RIB			
Shoulder		Épaule	
Shoulder cross rib roast	Cross rib pot roast, cross rib chuck roast	Rôti de côtes croisées	N/A (équivalent épaule + plat de côtes ficelé)
Short ribs	Braising short ribs, simmering short ribs	Côtes à braiser	Bouts de côtes, plat de côtes
Shoulder clod	Chuck shoulder clod	Pointe d'épaule	
Shoulder clod roast	Arm roast, clod roast, shoulder roast	Rôti de pointe d'épaule	
SHOULDER BLADE			
Shoulder blade		Haut côté (palette)	Côte découverte + épaule
Shoulder blade steak	Blade steak, shoulder blade chop	Côte découverte	Côte d'échine
Shoulder blade eye		OEil de palette	Jumeaux
Blade chuck roast	Blade pot roast, 7-bone chuck roast, 7-bone pot roast, bone-in chuck arm pot roast, bone-in chuck	Rôti de palette	Côtes découvertes + jumeaux + paleron avec os
Boneless blade chuck roast	Boneless blade pot roast, boneless chuck roast, boneless shoulder roast	Rôti de palette désossé	Côtes découvertes + jumeaux + paleron sans os
Flat iron	Top blade	Macreuse	Paleron
Shoulder bottom blade roast		Rôti de bas de palette	Côte découverte + épaule
Shoulder bottom blade steak	Shoulder bottom blade steak	Tranche de bas de palette	Tranche de côte découverte
Surprise steak		Surprise à griller	Surprise de veau
HEAD AND NECK			
Neck		Collier de veau	Collier
Sliced neck		Collier de veau tranché	Collier tranché
SHANK (FORE AND HIND)			
Frenched shank	Thor's hammer	Jarret à manchon	Jarret manchonné
Hindshank	Back shank	Jarret arrière	Jarret arrière
Foreshank	Front shank	Jarret avant	Jarret avant
Sliced shank	Osso buco, osso buco-style centre-cut shank	Jarret tranché	Jarret en tranche
SHOULDER BONE			
Shoulder bone		Os d'épaule	Une partie de l'épaule (coupe française)

NAMES OF **VEAL** CUTS

English	Alternate English	Quebec French	French
LOIN			
Loin		Longe	Longe (partie filet seulement)
Loin roast (with tenderloin)	Loin roast (with filet)	Rôti de longe avec filet	Rôti de longe française = partie filet seulement
Loin roast (without tenderloin)	Loin roast (without tenderloin)	Rôti de longe sans filet	Rôti de longe française (sans filet)
Loin chop	Veal T-bone	Côtelette filet	Côtelette filet/côtelette de longe
Tenderloin	Filet	Filet de veau	Filet/filet mignon
RIB			
Rack of veal	Rib roast, rib roast rack, hotel rack	Rôti de côtes	Rôti de côtes
Frenched rack of veal	Frenched rib roast, Frenched rib roast rack, Frenched hotel rack	Carré	Carré de veau manchonné
Crown roast	Rib crown roast, crown roast of veal	Couronne	Couronne
Rib chop (bone in, Frenched or not)	Cowboy chop	Côtes	Côte (première, haut de côte, seconde)
Tomahawk chop	Tomahawk, Frenched rib chop (with long bone)	Côte de veau manchon (os à blanc), Tomahawk de veau	Côte manchonnée
Ribeye roast (boneless)	Boneless rib roast	Rôti de faux-filet	
Hanger steak	Hanging tender	Onglet de veau	Onglet
FLANK			
Flank (primal cut)		Flanc nature	Tendron + flanchet
Flank steak		Flanc à griller de veau	Bavette de flanchet
Skirt steak		Hampe de veau	Hampe de veau
ROUND (BOTTOM, EYE, TOP)			
Outside leg	Leg bottom	Extérieur de cuisseau	Sous-noix
Outside leg roast	Leg bottom roast	Rôti d'extérieur de cuisseau	Rôti de sous-noix
Leg round steak		Tranche de cuisseau centre	
Eye of round (roast or steak)		Œil de ronde	Oeil
Inside leg	Top leg	Intérieur de cuisseau	La noix
Inside leg roast	Top leg roast	Rôti d'intérieur de cuisseau	Rôti de noix

NAMES OF **VEAL** CUTS

English	Alternate English	Quebec French	French
SIRLOIN TIP			
Sirloin tip		Pointe de surlonge	Noix pâtissière
Sirloin tip roast	Round tip roast, knuckle roast	Rôti pointe de surlonge (mouvant)	Mouvant noix pâtissière
Sirloin tip eye roast	Sirloin tip side roast, knuckle side roast	Rôti pointe de surlonge (plat)	Plat noix pâtissière
Sirloin tip round roast	Sirloin tip center roast, round tip roast cap-off, sirloin tip roast, knuckle center roast	Rôti pointe de surlonge (rond)	Rond noix pâtissière
HEEL OF ROUND			
Heel of round		Talon (talon de rouelle)	Talon
Banana shank	Red tail	La carotte (gousse d'ail de veau)	Galinette nerveux de gîte
SIRLOIN			
Sirloin		Surlonge	Quasi
Mouse steak		Langue de chat	Langue de chat
Spider steak		Araignée de veau	Araignée de veau
Top sirloin steak	Sirloin steak, top sirloin butt steak	Tranche de haut de surlonge	Tranche de quasi
Sirloin roast	Sirloin of veal, rump roast, standing sirloin roast (with bone)	Rôti de surlonge	Rôti de noix pâtissière
Bavette	Bottom sirloin flap, bottom sirloin bavette, flap meat	Bavette de veau	Bavette d'aloyau de veau
Tenderloin head	Tenderloin butt, butt tender, arrow head	Tête de filet	Filet partie tête
Coulotte (roast or steak)	Picanha (Brazil), top sirloin cap (roast or steak), sirloin cap (roast or steak), rump cap	Culotte de surlonge	Dessus de quasi
MISCELLANEOUS			
Kabob cubes	Cubes for skewers	Cubes à brochettes	Cubes à brochettes
Stew cubes	Cubes for stew, stewing cubes	Cubes à ragout	Cubes à mijoter
Paupiette	Stuffed bundles	Paupiette	Paupiette
Scaloppini	Escalopes	Escalope	Escalope
Strips	Stir-fry strips	Lanières	Émincés
Tenderized steak	Cubed steak, cube steak, minute steak, chicken fried steak, Swiss steak	Veau attendri	

NAMES OF **POULTRY** CUTS

English	Alternate English	Quebec French	French
Chicken		Poulet avec os et peau	Poulet
Cornish hen	Rock cornish, cornish game hen	Poulet de cornouailles	Poulet de cornouailles
Duck		Canard	Canard
Quail		Caille	Caille
Turkey		Dinde	Dinde
WHOLE			
Boneless whole chicken roast		Poulet désossé en rôti	Poulet complet en rôti, Poulet en ballotine
Boneless whole chicken, tied (with or without skin)	Melon-style boneless whole chicken	Poulet désossé façon melon	Poulet désossé attaché en melon
Stuffed boneless whole chicken, tied	Melon-style stuffed boneless whole chicken	Poulet désossé farci façon melon	Poulet désossé and farci attaché en melon
Spatchcocked chicken	Butterflied chicken, flattened chicken	Poulet papillon (Poulet en crapaudine)	
BREAST			
Split breast (with bone and skin)	Half breast (with bone and skin)	Demi-poitrine avec peau et os	Demi-poitrine sur coffre
Chicken chest	Whole breast on the bone, double breast on the bone	Poitrine complète (double) avec os et peau (Coffre de poulet)	Poitrine sur le coffre
Breast roast		Rôti de poitrine	Poitrine en rôti
Breast chop	Bone-in breast slice	Côtelette de pointrine (tranche avec os)	Côtelette de poitrine (avec os)
Boneless breast (with or without skin)		Demi-poitrine sans os sans peau	Filet, un blanc de poulet, Escalope de poulet
Stuffed breast		Poitrine farcie	Poitrine farcie
Chicken paupiette	Stuffed bundle	Paupiette	Paupiette
Breast tournedo	Bacon-wrapped chicken breast	Tournedos de poitrine	Filet de poulet bardé, Blanc de poulet bardé
Breast scaloppini	Cutlet	Escalope de poitrine	Blanc de poulet en escalope
Tender	Tenderloin, breast fillet	Filet	Aiguillette
LEG			
Bone-in leg quarter		Cuisse compléte	Cuisse
Oyster (along the spine)		Huître de poulet	Faux sol-l'y-laisse
Bone-in, skin-on leg without back		Cuisse sans dos avec os et peau	Cuisse sans dos
Boneless leg (with skin)		Cuisse désossée avec peau	Cuisse désossée avec peau
Stuffed boneless leg	Ballotine	Cuisse désossée farcie	Ballotine
Drumstick (with skin)		Pilon avec peau	Pilon
Butterflied drumstick (with bone open like a butterfly)		Pilon papillon (avec os ouvert en papillon)	

NAMES OF **POULTRY** CUTS

English	Alternate English	Quebec French	French
Stuffed boneless drumstick		Pilon désossé farci	Pilon désossé and farci, Pilon en ballotine
Frenched drumstick	Drumstick lollipop	Pilon manchon	Pilon manchonné
Stuffed Frenched drumstick	Stuffed drumstick lollipop	Pilon manchon farci	Pilon manchonné farci
Sliced drumstick	Poultry osso buco	Pilon désossé tranché	Pilon tranché, Pilon en osso buco
Thigh (with bone and skin)		Haut de cuisse avec os et peau	Haut de cuisse avec peau et os
Boneless, skinless thigh		Haut de cuisse désossé sans peau	Haut de cuisse sans peau sans os
WINGS			
Whole wing with bone and skin		Aile complète avec peau	Aile
Flat	Wingette	Médiane	La médiane
Drumette	Drum, wing drum	Pilon d'aile	Pilon
Wing tip		Pointe d'aile	Fouet
Whole wing, boneless		Aile complète désossée	Aile désossée
Split wing, flat and drumette	Split wing, wingette and drumette	Aile coupée	Fouet + manchon
MISCELLANEOUS			
Fondue (thin slices)	Poultry meat for fondue	Tranche à fondue	Volaille pour fondue ou pirade
Kabob cubes	Cubes for skewers	Cubes à brochettes	Cubes à brochettes
Cubes for stew	Stew cubes	Cubes à ragoût	Cube à mijoter
Strips		Lainères	Émincé
Chicken feet		Pied de poulet	Patte
DUCK			
Duck magret	Breast of Moulard duck (with or without bone)	Magret (canard gavé)	Magret de canard
Duck breast		Poitrine de canard (non gavé)	Poitrine de canard
RABBIT			
Saddle		Râble de lapin	Râble
Front legs		Raquettes de lapin	Gigolettes

OSTEOLOGY

QUADRUPEDS

CARNIVORE

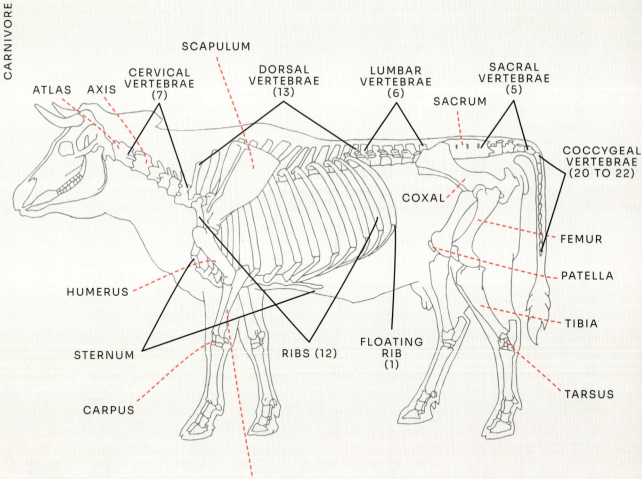

ATLAS AXIS

CERVICAL VERTEBRAE (7)

SCAPULUM

DORSAL VERTEBRAE (13)

LUMBAR VERTEBRAE (6)

SACRAL VERTEBRAE (5)

SACRUM

COCCYGEAL VERTEBRAE (20 TO 22)

COXAL

FEMUR

PATELLA

TIBIA

HUMERUS

STERNUM

RIBS (12)

FLOATING RIB (1)

CARPUS

TARSUS

RADIUS + ULNA

CARTILAGE + QUALITY ZONES

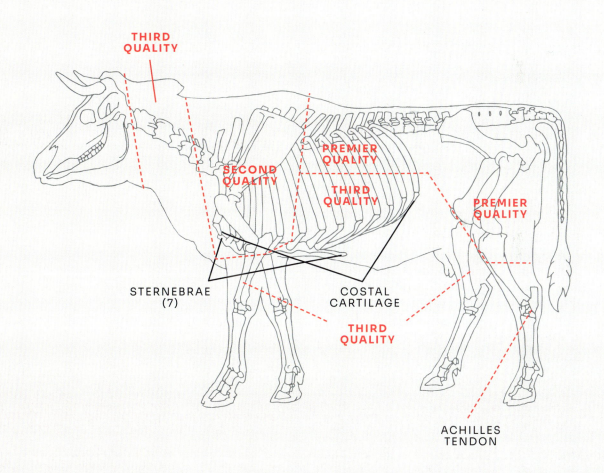

QUADRUPEDS

THIRD
QUALITY

PREMIER
QUALITY

SECOND
QUALITY

THIRD
QUALITY

PREMIER
QUALITY

STERNEBRAE
(7)

COSTAL
CARTILAGE

THIRD
QUALITY

ACHILLES
TENDON

OSTEOLOGY

POULTRY

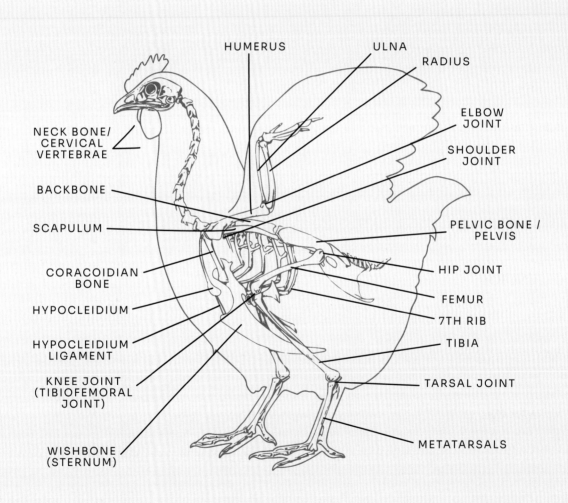

HUMERUS

ULNA

RADIUS

ELBOW JOINT

SHOULDER JOINT

NECK BONE/ CERVICAL VERTEBRAE

BACKBONE

SCAPULUM

PELVIC BONE / PELVIS

HIP JOINT

CORACOIDIAN BONE

FEMUR

HYPOCLEIDIUM

7TH RIB

HYPOCLEIDIUM LIGAMENT

TIBIA

KNEE JOINT (TIBIOFEMORAL JOINT)

TARSAL JOINT

METATARSALS

WISHBONE (STERNUM)

ACKNOWLEDGMENTS

All those who supported me – you are wonder-FOWL:

Claudia Clément (producer, Trio orange)
Without Claudia, you would not be holding this book in your hands today. Claudia, thank you for talking to me about the book, which was just a vague idea at the time, and bringing it to Les Éditions de l'Homme. You believed in the project and in its potential even before I believed in it 100% myself.

Les Éditions de l'Homme
Huge thanks to **Sophie Aumais** (editorial director) for getting on board with my irascible carnivore girl project! Thank you for believing in my dream and helping me make it come true with a fantastic group of people: **Marianne Prairie** (editor), **Chantal Legault** (food stylist), **Ariel Tarr** (photographer), **Christine Hébert** (art director), **Clémence Beaudoin** (graphic designer) and all those who worked on this book in one way or another. Thank you!

Claudine Roy (French teacher)
An **ENORMOUS** thank you to my former high school French teacher (in secondaire 3, when I was 14)! Who would have thought that 20 years later, she would still be telling me the same things (ha-ha!). Thank you for helping me to correct these texts over and over . . . giving me hours and hours of your personal time. I am grateful for your incredible commitment to building this book one page at a time. Thank you to my writing partner in crime! xox

Support from some VEAL-ly great butchers:

Grinder butcher shop (1654 Notre-Dame Ouest, Montreal)
Thanks, boys (**Charles Bizeul**, **Sarto Chartierotis**, **Jean-François Corriveau**), for lending me your beautiful butcher shop so I could have THE most amazing cover photo in the most gorgeous meat fridge in Montreal!

Pascal le boucher butcher shop (8113 Saint-Denis, Montreal)
Thank you, **Pascal Hudon**, for lending me your acclaimed and magnificent butcher shop essentially unsupervised so I could take great photos for the book. Thank you so much for your trust and your massive help to make this project a reality!

Massive thanks also to **Gabriel Roy** (butcher at Pascal le boucher), with whom I did my butcher's course in 2014. Gab, thank you for that day of preparing some gorgeous cuts to photograph (and for giving up your day off for us, ha-ha!). You were all in with this project, and I really appreciate your help!

Brad Mcleod (butchery professor, Olds College of Agriculture & Technology, Alberta): Thank you for teaching me A TON of butchering concepts *in English*. Five years ago, you and your wife were visiting Montreal. I invited you for a smoked meat sandwich at Schwartz's after I finished work . . . Five years later, you were there to help me, and I am so grateful. Thanks, my friend!

La boucherie du marché butcher shop (224 place du Marché-du-Nord, Montreal): Thank you, **Patrick Loyau**, for letting me improve my French butchering technique, surrounded by three incredibly qualified French butchers (**Benoit Fessy**, **Aurélien Frontella**, **Lionel Frelin**) for several years.

Bernard Flamant (retired retail butchery professor, École hôtelière de Montréal): Thank you to my butchery professor as well as to the École hôtelière de Montréal for having shared with me, with pleasure and joy, the knowledge I needed to become a butcher and write this book 10 years later!

Thank you, **Sarah-Maude St-Laurent** (Ferme éco'land des basques cattle farm, Trois-Pistoles), for visits to the farm to talk about raising beef as well as butchering between us girls.

Very DEER friends and family:

Thank you, **Gabrielle Joubert**, for finding me a duck breast at 10 p.m. when I needed one for 6 o'clock the next morning, ha-ha!

And thanks to **Sam Di Tommaso**, who brought me a dried pork tenderloin at the speed of light at work so I could photograph that recipe while I was working.

Caroline Houle, my neighbor who me loaned me her outdoor space for the BBQ photos: thanks so much!

Kevin Lecavalier, **Gabriel Gauthier**, my two biggest supporters whom I can always count on: thanks!

Sanelli (the whole family!): thank you for always making sure my knives are sharp . . . and for m'en avoir fait des ROSES!

Huge thanks to my father (**Bertrand Rioux**), my brother (**Laurent Rioux**), my mother (**Lise Beaumier**) and my best friend (**Jean-Paul Phillipe Thériault**). You have helped me so much, each in your own way, to make a childhood dream come true: write a book! I love you xox.

Special thanks to my pet cat, **Chopine**, who was purring at my side for the entire writing of this book, even during TEAMs MEAT-ings.

INDEX